SECRETS OF BREATH

You Can Have What You Want – The Ultimate Life Changer

SECRETS OF BREATH

You Can Have What You Want – The Ultimate Life Changer

RAJEEV SAXENA

Translated by **AASHA KHOSA**

PRABHAT PRAKASHAN

Published by
PRABHAT PRAKASHAN PVT. LTD.
4/19 Asaf Ali Road,
New Delhi-110002 (INDIA)
e-mail: prabhatbooks@gmail.com

ISBN 978-93-5521-198-9
SECRETS OF BREATH
by Rajeev Saxena

Edition
2025

Price
₹ 450 (Rupees Four Hundred Fifty Only)

Printed at
R-Tech Offset Printers, Delhi

Dedicated to my Baba
who inspired me to write this book.

Preface

Breathing is life and yet we never pay attention to it. It is really none of our business to interfere in a vital life process that, we believe, is happening anyway, on its own. Something inside us keeps it going till our end.

Do a small experiment: consciously stop breathing for a few seconds. Suddenly you will realise your mind has gone blank; thoughts have vanished, and it remains so till you can hold your breath. The book explores the intrinsic relation between breathing and our mind, body, and consciousness.

Author Rajeev Saxena's account is based on his Sadhna. In the spiritual lexicon, Sadhna is not learning or understanding and probably English has no matching word for it. It refers to an exercise within you with your breath as the only tool for experiencing concepts given in the ancient Indian texts.

Notwithstanding the style, in essence, the book is a Do-it-yourself (DIY) project on facilitating mundane life. It gives you step by step procedure on how to make a business meeting successful just by shifting your posture and breathing consciously; tips on how to endear yourself to others or get rid of unwanted people in your life. You can even know how to sense the impending disease and prevent it or travel safe etc. In fact, through regulated and conscious breathing, it is possible to even arrest ageing and prolong the life span!

I must share my experience of translating this book with the readers. As soon as I got a grip over the subject, I knew I had embarked on a journey of self-discovery. It started with a realisation that despite having graduated in biology, I didn't know some basic facts about the human body. For example, I never studied that humans breathe out heavily from one nostril at a given time and this regimen changes every hour. I discovered it from the book through self-testing that it prescribes in most situations.

Such simple and stark facts explained with logic make this book addictive. During the writing of this book, I would suddenly have an urge to check my Nadi.

Sometimes, I felt it needed a course correction and would quickly go through the chapter on how to change the Nadi. It turned out to be a simple exercise and worked well! Like they say in Disneyland, the employees go on their knees to speak with visitors – children, in that case – the author has taken care to demystify concepts related to spiritualism with infallible reasoning to make sure the reader does not feel overwhelmed by the esoteric subject.

The book shatters the myth of breathing not being our business. The Chapter on the secrets of breathing explains why we should take charge of our breathing.

This understanding opens a mine of possibilities in front of readers. You will realise that being in charge of your breathing is important. After taking charge, you would discover your vast innate strength to control events in your life, turn failures into successes, live in happiness and harmony with nature. Breathing with awareness leads you to the path of your soul's journey and is the real mantra for a happy and contented life.

Human beings are a tiny speck in the scheme of things of nature. Because of this, our body rhythms are synchronised with the movement of celestial bodies.

However, the modern-day lifestyle has hugely disrupted this rhythm. This out of sync body-nature equation can be checked simply through easy self-examinations; the corrections suggested are also equally easy to follow.

The mind of a human being is created by senses and his intellect grows with experience. However, this overt power that humans often boast of is not even an iota of our inner power that lays dormant due to our lack of awareness and living in a state of unconsciousness. The chapter on Mind and consciousness will make you wonder about the potential of a human being; search for real ecstasy within your inner-self.

The Book will be a great practical guide to the young men and women who have aspirations and goals and yet they often falter because of the distractions of the world.

It has changed my perception about life, myself and the world; made me a calmer and happier human being.

I feel empowered on realising I can change many things in life through simple breathing techniques and living with awareness.

The author's style of explaining the otherwise complex concepts is convincing and charming. The path of spiritualism is not an uphill climb to a Himalayan peak; it can be practised as we move around in the material world performing our responsibilities and yet at heart remaining as detached from the ephemeral material world as a mendicant.

I am sure the book can only enrich and improve the quality of your life as it has done for me.

–AASHA KHOSA
Sr. Journalist

Prologue

Breath is not merely a sign of life; it is complementary to and the propeller of life. Our breath is behind all reactions happening inside our body.

Even outside, in the mundane world, all that happens to us is linked to the breath. Both peace of mind and lack of it are linked to the breath.

Breath is behind our thoughts, choice of food, business and work-related decisions; the melancholy that overwhelms us when we suffer losses in life or the ecstasies of making it big. In fact, all that happens in our lives and the outcomes of our actions or interactions are not only related to the breath but also because of it. It is responsible for all our troubles and also about those that we have managed to prevent.

The subtle reactions in our breath are behind our ill- health or approaching death. The same is also behind our emotion of anger, hate, frustration or jealousy.

When a human being is happy, in love or in a state of bliss these reactions make an about-turn. It is true though difficult to believe that the pattern of breathing and subtle reactions in the breath of a man and a woman at the time of copulation determines the characteristics of the child to be born out of the union.

Having knowledge about breath can help us manage our problems. Again, it can help us have the focus of mind and do Dhyana. Our actions that are compatible with the chemistry of our breath will end in success.

The science of breath makes breathing an involuntary action. Our breath has a direct link with the sun and the moon. The impact of these celestial bodies on our breath is a natural phenomenon; it is as precise as Newton's laws of motion. Like nature, the breath is pregnant with myriad mysteries. This science is a piece of rare and ancient knowledge.

This book gives an interesting account of the science of breathing and explains how one can learn it. Why should one ignore breathing? Let's learn how its knowledge can make miracles happen.

RAJEEV SAXENA

❑

Introduction

Adarsh Khanna

Retd. Professor and head of department, National Council of Educational Research and Training (NCERT), New Delhi. Formerly: Curriculum consultant to World Bank, Washington, USA; Curriculum Advisor to UNESCO for Bangladesh, Dhaka; Curriculum Consultant to UNICEF, Bangladesh and Nepal; Consultant (Female education) Rockefeller Foundation, New York, USA.

I have read the draft of the book. Though I had some knowledge about breathing, the secrets of breathing unraveled in this book are beyond my imagination. I was amazed to realize that breathing is so important in our normal life as well as in our journey to pinnacle of spirituality. In fact this book is a great resource on questions related to the art of self-exploration.

Little is known about the fact that Sun and Moon have a direct impact on each of our breath. Not many people know that breathing has an impact on all events in our life. We seldom realise that all our failures and successes are linked to our breath. This book will help the readers understand the intrinsic link between breathing and all aspects of our life.

The book presents knowledge in easy, simple and interesting ways. The style of writing is very impressive and original. Both young and old, ranging from 14 years to the elderly readers will find the book interesting and useful. The basis of this book is the ancient science of swara.

The opening chapter is alluring; readers will be motivated to delve into the next chapter. Each chapter evokes curiosity in the mind of reader to know more. The book is based on experiences of the author. The narrative keeps reader glued to the book; his mind glides through the book.

The chapter "The Way to Success" is simple narrative. Do it yourself tip can be easily followed in our daily routine. The chapter "How to Feel Nadi?" is also quite easy to follow. The chapter "The length of the breath" gives easy and useful tips. "Flow of Tatva in Our Body"demands a thorough understanding followed by a rigorous practice. Chapter on "Astrology and Science of Nadi" is a sure shocker for readers both with faith in astrology and others. Every fact is enumerated on scientific basis.

"Sadhna and breathing" gives precise and lucid knowledge that can clear our doubts on many issues. Every sentence of chapter "You Can Control The World" made me quip, "This is absolutely true". It was the same with the entire chapter and at the end I was asking myself, "How come I didn't know these and the fact about the power of human mind?" The next chapter "Seven Levels of Mind" had answers to my queries. The chapter "The Wandering Mind" imparts rare knowledge and that in turn prepares you for the next one. The last chapter "Chakra Sadhna"gives easy to do method to raise your energy from Mooladhar Chakra to Sahasrara chakra.

I have lost count of the books I have read both in Hindi and English. I can say with confidence that this book is not the one that can be shelved after reading. As and when a reader decides to use the rare knowledge in the book for practice to change his life, he/she would have to turn its pages again and again. The knowledge given in the book if practiced has the potential to change one's life completely.

My Best Wishes to Rajeev,

– **Adarsh Khanna**

Contents

PART I-THE BREATH

1

CHAPTER

How I Discovered This Knowledge?

I have been a journalist for over 30 years. As an editor with newspapers and news magazines, I tracked events and potential newsmakers every day. Amidst such a hectic lifestyle, spirituality was, apparently, the last thing in my mind. So, today when I look back at my life 20 years ago – people who knew me back then would vouch for me – I feel, my present-day inclination towards spirituality is a miracle.

The irony is that at the beginning of my career, I wrote many stories about the so-called Babas – the men selling cures, miracles, hopes and skills in the name of religion to the poor and incredulous. It was a world with no television in India. Newspapers and news magazines enjoyed credibility and a reverential readership; the published stories made an impact. My stories on the Babas exposed many of them for exploiting masses in the name of religion; readers appreciated these.

As I researched and wrote more such stories, my belief that most of them were charlatans and exploiters was confirmed. Honestly, I could never imagine that one day I will take one of them as my Guru. I wondered if these Babas were genuine mystics then why they lived amidst mundane chaos; they could have gone to the Himalaya for Sadhna in its splendid solitude.

Today, my experience has made me realise that we should never form opinions on hearsay or under the influence of others. However, back then as I was busy with work and had no time to reflect on such issues.

Since the year 2003, my life has drastically changed; today I am deeply interested in spirituality. I do not discuss it with others and it is known only to my family and a few close friends.

In the year 2000, a friend took me to Ramakrishna Mission in Delhi for learning meditation. It was my first tryst with meditation. After that visit, I would often sit with closed eyes for hours. I had no particular purpose for this. In fact, sometimes I wondered if I was wasting my time.

Three years later, my life was to change.

I was in Mumbai for planning the launch of India's first tabloid on the social life of celebrities, high society and the rich and the famous. I often travelled to Mumbai from Delhi. On that particular day, I was staying in the Marriott Hotel. My friend who accompanied me wanted me to meet one of his acquaintances. He described him as a landowner from Pune, West India, who was facing a financial crisis. "Sometimes he does behave like a weird person", my friend warned me. My job was to interact with him and give my honest feedback to my friend.

"I want to help him in case you find him reliable", my friend briefed me beforehand. Let me confess, back then, I was confident in my power to judge a person just by looking at his face.

"Sure, it's no big deal; call him", I told my friend, with unmistaken bravado.

He was a 6-foot, clean-shaven man with a glow on his face. Dressed in a half-sleeve white kurta and pyjamas, he came to my hotel room. After exchanging pleasantries, I ordered tea for him. As he sipped tea, I asked him, "Why didn't you think of selling the land or mortgaging it to secure a bank loan to tide over the crisis?"

He was silent as the gaze of his bright eyes remained fixed on me, making me somewhat uncomfortable. "That land is no longer mine; I have donated it to my Guru Maharaj", he said in a soft voice.

Here I was meeting yet another credulous man who had fallen to the charms of a charlatan Baba. The tall-man's calm demeanour remained unchanged. I curtly asked him", "Why did you transfer the land to your Guru and put yourself in trouble?"

He was unmoved by my outburst. The journalist inside me was sensing a news story unfolding: yet another charlatan Baba has defrauded a rich man of his property. It surely was an explosive story, I told myself.

"There is no registry (papers of transfer of land's ownership) in Baba's name. He asked for it and I gave away".

Again, I must have sounded brash, "How can you give away your land to somebody without making a registry?" I was done with him and didn't want to ask him more questions. He was insane, I told myself.

The tall-man suddenly folded his hands to me and said, "How can one give to the Guru; it is the Guru who gives everything. I merely obeyed my Guru when he wanted the land. Now, the land belongs to him". He smiled and there was no hint of sarcasm in his tone. This time, his expression suddenly made me conscious of my inadequacies. Did I hear him say, "You fool, you won't understand?"

As he rose to leave, I couldn't help ask him, "Where can I meet your Guru?" He told me that just three days ago, his Guru had taken Samadhi. That means the Guru had buried himself under the soil to prepare for his soul to leave the world. The 118-year old Guru had done it consciously and wilfully. "Now, it's my turn to become an ascetic and renounce the world. I need the money to pay of some debts", he said and left.

He was strange and yet I could not take my mind of him. After he was gone, I was reliving my experience with him. In between, I also thought about his Guru. Didn't taking a Samadhi amount to committing suicide? Is it right for someone to end his life and still be revered as a Guru?

I and my friend was invited by a real estate builder to his house in Kandivali for dinner. As we entered, I spotted the tall-man sitting in a chair in a corner of the large drawing-room. There were a lot of people around. Our conversation was generally around Bhagavad Gita. Everyone was flaunting his knowledge of the Book and speaking like scholars. The tall-man was silently listening to it; after some time, he interjected: "Your perception about the Gita is not correct; all ancient texts including Gita have metaphorical references".

I was drawn to him as others paid no attention to what he said. I turned to him and asked a question about the Gita. As he was giving me a detailed answer, I wanted him to finish fast so that I can throw another question at him. Basically, instead of listening to him, I was judging him. To my utter surprise, before I asked him the question, he started answering it.

How did he know what I was thinking of ? Maybe it was a coincidence, I told myself. This pattern continued; I never got an opportunity to speak and put my questions to him, and yet hc was answering all. To the others, it seemed like a boring monologue, and they showed no interest in it. For me, it was an intense conversation. I didn't care about dinner and asked my friend to go ahead with it.

For me, it was a life-changing conversation and we continued till 5 am; others had gone to sleep while the two of us didn't even have a proper meal. My curiosity was insatiable and questions were never-ending. I felt guilty of judging him in haste; I had erred.

His words trickled deep down in my mind, scrapping out my preconceived notions about life. I could feel this process. With a masters' degree in chemistry, he explained Bhagwad Gita logically and with the clarity of a scientist's mind. To me, it was an extraordinary experience. I had never met an erudite man, whose knowledge of things prodded my curiosity to no end.

Interestingly, he often prefixed all his answers with "By the grace of my Baba". I asked him about his Guru. "Baba (his Guru) has no name. He had renounced everything; people believed he was a madman. So, everybody called him 'Khapti Baba'. (Khapti, a colloquial term for an eccentric or a madman)

Khapti Baba was born in a low-income family in a remote village of district Amravati, Maharashtra. He left his home in early childhood and therefore had never attended a school. After spending many years in the jungle, he returned to his village where locals were shocked to see a naked man with an emaciated body covered in soil and having long and matted hair. They were scared of him and ran away at his sight. They called him khapti (madman)".

"How can one find a genuine Guru?" I asked him.

He said, "If a seeker is qualified to judge a Guru, then he does not need one! A genuine Guru is not a magician who can pull stuff out of the thin air; he makes you feel his presence that too only if he decides to".

He suddenly asked me I had any experience with Baba. I was searching for appropriate words to frame a diplomatic reply as he said, "A Guru doesn't care about respect and disrespect; he is above such things".

How did he know that I faced a dilemma in answering him so that I don't sound irreverent? Was it a sheer coincidence, again?

"How could I feel his presence when I had never seen Baba?" I told him.

He smiles and said, "Samadhi does not mean that Baba is no more. His body was old, so he left it; he is with us right now. He is a free soul. If he wishes, you might experience his presence".

My obsession with the tall-man was annoying for others. Though I felt sleepy, I wanted the conversation to continue. We ended it only in the wee hours after I suddenly remembered about my flight to Delhi the same day. I instinctively felt like touching his feet to show my respect, and as I bent, he quipped, "Oh! What are you doing?"

He gave me a picture of his Guru."If you wish, you can keep it", he said. I shoved it in my wallet and left. Back in my hotel room, I could not sleep; the tall-man's words echoed in my mind. I wondered how a well-to-do, highly educated person, with a fantastic knowledge of the Gita, had chosen an illiterate man as his Guru. In high school, I had studied the life story of Sant Kabir, a 15th century spiritual Guru, who was uneducated. This probably means that 'real knowledge' has nothing to do with schooling!

So many questions were popping up in my mind.

On the way to the airport, I felt restless. I had to board a flight to Delhi, my home, and yet something was bothering me. I was overwhelmed by a desire to meet the tall-man and talk to him incessantly. Those days, I would frequently travel between Delhi and Mumbai for the tabloid project. Maybe I can meet him on my next visit. I had reached the airport and suddenly I had decided to stay back. I saw my friend off at the airport and returned to the city, checking into another seaside hotel.

I called another friend, the publisher of our proposed tabloid and owner of a social club. I wanted her to take me to the tall-man. Since I was not familiar with Mumbai roads, she would help me. She was at Nariman point and could reach me only in two hours. I decided to spend time in the sea-facing open-air restaurant in the hotel.

The restaurant had only two customers. After ordering sandwiches and tea, I took out the picture of Khapti Baba from my wallet and looked at it carefully.

The Baba was sitting on a leopard skin in Padmasana. With his small unkempt beard and a red shawl wrapped around his chest, he looked very much a common villager and hardly like a Guru.

I looked at the sea. I saw a void, a kind of vacant and peaceful nothing. I suddenly lost the sense of my being and surroundings. I was in a dream-like state and saw the funeral pyres of some of the members of my family burning. I also saw some scenes from my past life.

It was an extraordinary experience!

"Sir... Sir... Sir", the loud voice of the waiter woke me up. "Your phone has been ringing!"

I had come back from wherever I had got transported to. My friend had arrived in her car and she was frantically calling me.

"Sorry, I think I had dozed of", I tried to address the waiter's bewilderment.

"Sir, I had been calling you for quite some time, you opened your eyes and didn't respond. I also served you sandwiches and tea but you haven't touched these". I quickly paid the bill and left in my friend's car without addressing his concerns.

Honestly, this experience had scared me to the core. As my friend drove to tall-man's place, I told her about it. She thought I was hallucinating, probably due to lack of sleep. I was not convinced; my experience had nothing to do with lack of sleep.

I narrated my experience to the tall-man. He too seemed to think it was due to sleep deprivation. I was a bit disappointed as his reaction failed to address my fearful anxiety. I had probably failed to explain it properly to him. I was not able to concentrate on anything. In the process, I simply forgot the reasons that made me cancel my flight. At the end of the meeting, he suggested me to read two books, Vivek Chudamani and Panchadashi.

Back in Delhi, I kept thinking about my Juhu beach experience. However, after a few days, life became normal. I got busy with my job and the routine. I bought both books. These were about Upanishads. I tried to read them but somehow could not move beyond a few pages. I did my best to get interested in the book. Somehow my logical mind failed to comprehend the hidden meanings in the text.

Six months later we met again. He had called me to a roadside teashop in Mumbai's Kandivali. My anxiety got better of me and I asked him to take me as his disciple. He started laughing incessantly and said, "It is easy to accept someone as a master, but difficultto become a true disciple. I am only a disciple; not a master". He also asked if I had read the books.

I told him that I could not understand the content of the books and, therefore, left them halfway. As I was explaining my problem with the book, he smiled and said, "You are an editor of a major newspaper and intelligent enough. What is in the books that you didn't understand?"

"Babuji, I tried hard: it's difficultto understand the meaning". I had instinctively addressed him as Babuji (Like a father, in Hindi). He had a hearty laugh and said, "Well, try once more. Maybe, this time you will understand".

I asked him more about his Guru Khapti Baba; I told him I was thinking of writing a story about him in my newspaper. He said the Baba may not like the publicity and may hurl filthy abuses on me on knowing about it.

"Are saints allowed to hurl abuses?" I asked him. He said he had been listening to the abuses (from his Guru) for 20 years and always took them as blessings. He was not sure if he was permitted to call names and laughed loudly.

Thereafter he narrated many stories from Khapti Baba's life. The most interesting one was about a diamond merchant of Surat, who came to him with a wish. The husband of trader's only daughter was paralysed. The family had consulted doctors across India and abroad and yet nothing happened. The trader's son-in-law was completely bed-ridden. One day the merchant came to know about Khapti Baba and he took the ailing man to him. His daughter also came along.

Baba had no ashram or a permanent dwelling. The family randomly inquired from the locals about Baba's location. They reached a tea shop in a village in Yavatmal. It was right on the edge of a forest. The tea stall owner told the trader that Baba had just left for the forest.

The family had come a long way from Surat and yet there was no chance of meeting the Baba. "When will Baba come next?" he asked the stall owner.

"No one knows. Only when Baba wishes, he comes".

Khapti Baba

That was disappointing and yet the businessman decided to spend the night out in the open as there was no other place to stay. His paralysed son-in-law was carried from Surat on a cot that he lay on. Others slept on the grassy patch in a deserted place. The merchant was disappointed and was planning to return home the next morning. The family had lost all hope of meeting the Baba.

In the wee hours, the merchant and his daughter were packing to return when they heard the low cries of help of the paralysed man, "Oh God, please save me!"

Everyone looked in the direction of where he lay on the cot. To their utter shock and surprise, Khapti Baba was there. He was mercilessly beating the sick man with a stick. Both of them ran to save him.

What happened next was unbelievable. The young man jumped out of the cot and started running to save himself from Baba's beatings!

Everyone saw him hop into a stationary bus. It was a moment of joy for them as they realised Baba had cured him.

The merchant and his daughter touched Baba's feet and cried, "Baba ki Jai ho" (Hail the Baba). Khapti Baba was hardly amused. He held the lathi (stick) in his hand and ran after the father-daughter duo, yelling, "Since you were just waiting for the dawn to leave, you better get lost".

I had always thought the Babas are offered cash by devotees in lieu of favours or granting of wishes, but here was a man who was going to beat up those who wanted to thank him for a miracle.

I was wondering why such a selfless person needs Babuji's land.

It seems Khapti Baba could demand anything from his followers, but not even touch or look back at it.

Likewise, Babuji's fertile and yielding land given to Baba was untouched and had turned into a mini forest with cattle and animals grazing. Baba never saw it even once. The truth is that Baba had no needs for anything and could even go without food for days.

Once he made Babuji buy a rickety truck for ₹50,000. Later, Babuji realised that the former truck owner had used the money to marry his three daughters. The truck had remained unused.

Once, a politician from Bihar, Lalu Prasad Yadav, came to meet Khapti Baba. He was accompanied by a retinue of followers. Yadav told Baba he had come for his darshan. Baba replied in Marathi, "Have you come for my darshan or giving yours".

These stories made me fall in love with Baba. In my mind, I re-lived my Juhu beach experience. I was no longer terrified of Baba's aura; my heart was filled with nothing but warmth and gratitude towards him.

Babuji again reminded me to read the books.

I tried to read one of the books before going to bed and got stuck in a word "Prakriti" (Nature). To me, a particular sentence with this word made no sense. Then, something happened and I suddenly read 'Mind' for "Prakriti" and it made perfect sense. I finished reading the book that night and enjoyed it thoroughly. Just an idea had turned the situation around me. It made me realise the importance of an idea as a life tool.

This was a life-changing incident for me. I suddenly lost interests in attending parties in Mumbai as part of my new job as editor of the tabloid.

Holding polite conversations with random people of high-pitched political debates was no longer my cup of tea. It all sounded hollow and meaningless.

Ups and Downs

On Babuji's advice, I read ancient texts like Geeta, Kathopanishada, Mundak Upanishada and Chhandogya Upanishada etc. Each book unravelled the same truth in a different manner. I was naive to believe in the power of my half-baked knowledge. Being proud of one's knowledge is real ignorance. Shivasutra says it so aptly: "Gyanam Bandha Kala Shariram", knowledge is a human being's biggest hurdle to reach the real truth.

As Babuji never showed an inclination to take me as his disciple, I turned to Baba. I would sit in a quiet corner of my house, look at his picture and speak with him. He generously granted all my 'genuine' wishes. I took him as my grandfather. During our conversations, I was never conscious of his stature as a Mahatma (great soul).

One day, I suddenly received a call from Babuji. He was coming to Delhi and to stay at my place. I received him at the airport. As per his directions, I had bought a coconut and a towel for him. Additionally, I also bought material for a kurta-pyjama as a token offering. My wish was granted; he took me as his disciple.

In a quiet corner of my house, Babuji first taught me the right way to sit on a Siddhasana. Next, he explained the use of elements of breath for "Soham". In the end, he imparted a mantra for regular chanting. This is called Guru mantra; the disciple has to keep it as a secret all his life. He also gave me tips on how to focus on the breath. I had a fixed morning routine. He clearly told me to stick to this and attempt no other practice. Babuji said from then onwards, he was directly responsible for me, his first disciple.

I sincerely followed this regimen for two years. I would sit in dhyana for three hours at a stretch and yet never had an experience. I was getting restless and told Babuji about it. As always, he dismissed it and asked me to focus on my routine.

Though I continued my Sadhna, peace eluded my mind. Instead, it was seething with questions about my inner journey–spiritualism. I was perturbed and started writing the questions for Babuji. I was desperate to meet him.

Babuji always parried my questions. My every visit to Amravati to meet him cost me about Rs 40,000. My purpose was to seek answers from him to myriad questions nagging me. He received me with the affection of a mother. However, each time I broached upon the subject, he spoke about food and what should be the day's menu. In fact, Babuji himself was a great cook.

Babuji made me sit next to him and asked about my life. Thereafter, all the talk initiated by him was about food. After breakfast, he would discuss the menu for lunch and then for dinner. He took me to the field in Amravati where he often plucked fruit and offered it to me said, "This will never taste the same in Delhi or Mumbai".

I returned all the more frustrated and anxious. After all, I had spent money on travel and boarding and taken leave from work to meet Babuji and find answers to my questions. I didn't come here just to eat and talk about food. Though sometime after dinner he answered a couple of questions to cheer me up. Babuji read my mind and see the next question coming. He quickly closed the conversation by saying, "I will explain this to you in detail later".

For the next five months, I didn't meet Babuji. His phone was always not reachable. I sent my friends to look for him in Mumbai and Amravati without any success. I was upset and felt like a rudderless boat. The publisher of our tabloid could understand my plight.

Intending to help me, she told me about her sister-in-law, who had been practising dhyana for 12 years.

One year had passed without any contact with Babuji.

Much later I realised that Babuji had gone to Narmada for Tapasya and remained incommunicado. I had lost all hope of meeting him and decided to hop on to the next available bandwagon to continue my journey. I met my friend's sister-in-law the next day. She was married and lived with her family. In our first meeting, I took her as my sister and addressed her as 'Behna'.

Here I need to explain that one can choose among four Marga (paths) to spiritual attainment: Gyan marg (path of knowledge), Yoga marg, Bhakti marg (Devotion) and Tantra marg (this should not be mixed with exorcism). Baba and Babuji had opted for the Gyan marg and yoga. The path of Bhakti (devotion) involves purification and evolution of mind. The path of Yoga empowers one with control over the body as a way to attain spiritual heights. Behna was from Aghori communion about which not much is known.

Aghoris are mostly mistaken for a cult whose members live in crematoriums and are believed to eat their excreta. People are generally afraid of them. In reality, Aghor is linked to the tantra path. I was keen to know more about this communion from Behna. She always sat on a red blanket covered with a red sheet; she held a Rudraksha rosary in her hand before settling down for dhyana. We had lively conversations; unlike Babuji she never dampened my curiosity by giving snappy replies to my questions.

I was happy at my association with Behna. I thought maybe she would guide me in the absence of Babuji; maybe the red cloth asana was a better way. I asked her whether I should also use a red blanket and a Rudraksha. She told me to consult my Guru (Babuji). Finally, I started using the red blanket and other tips she gave me for Sadhna. I felt better as I mixed Babuji's instructions with Behna's tips. She would ask me to meet her often.

Meanwhile, I never gave up my search for Babuji. I knew he would be happy with my experiment. One day, I finally received a call from him. He was coming to Delhi. With childlike excitement, I told him about Behna and my new experiment. He listened to me with his characteristic demeanour.

After some time, I was at the receiving end of his anger. He looked sad and spoke to me in a harsh tone, "I tried to teach you to descend like a crane from the skies for picking the food; you chose to be like a squirrel that stealthily climbs a tree to steal fruit".

I tried to explain my position. I told him that since I was not able to get in touch with him my anxiety took me to Behna. However, I had never given up the route that he had charted for me. He gave me a patient hearing. "If one is thirsty and water is not available for sometimes, can one drink kerosene?" he asked.

I had realised my mistake. Babuji told me that one must tread the path that one has chosen. Changing paths midway only furthers the destination. Thereafter, I never digressed from the path Babuji had put me on. Dhyana became a routine like bathing, getting ready, eating etc. With each passing day, my mind was at peace; there was no anxiety. Dhyana happened to me. Yes, it is true: dhyana does not come with rigorous practice or efforts; it happens. It happens when the mind becomes calm. In turn, the calm mind reaches a state of emptiness and it stops working.

Slowly, answers to questions that had troubled me started coming up during my stage of Dhyana. I got all answers to my satisfaction. The remaining unanswered questions never bothered me. However, I still had one unresolved question: how come I got all my answers.

I asked Babuji about this mystery. He said, "A Guru is always in touch with his disciple. He first tests his resolve and later takes charge of chiselling and gives him all he deserves. There is no need to convey it through speech. If I tell you something (answers to questions) it will be I speaking and not your experience. A Guru always makes a disciple self-reliant".

I broke down and touched his feet in reverence. "What should I do now?" I asked him. "You don't have to do anything: Baba will get things done through you".

Today, 15 years later, I do not meet Babuji often yet I never miss him. He and Baba are always with me and I can feel their presence. I do my Sadhna. For months together I do not speak to Babuji and yet I do not feel we are living apart.

Gradually I started experiencing the subtle reactions in my breath during my practices and Dhyana. I did exactly as I was told: just kept my focus on breathing and indeed the secrets did tumble out.

Later I met a Saint, whom I call Acharyaji. He gave me a lot of knowledge about breathing. I did practice on the lines of the new concepts.

I dedicate the knowledge of the science of breathing and consciousness that I acquired from Baba and Babuji before offering it to the readers for consumption and use to make their lives better.

I bow in reverence to the creators of ancient texts, the Swara Shastras.

RECAP

- Some Godmen perform miracles like pulling a gold chain from thin air while others create holy ash from their palms. This is magic and should be left to the magicians; they can perform it better.

- How do we differentiate between a spiritual Guru and a charlatan?

- One can never judge a Guru. If someone is capable of doing it, he would not need a Guru.

- Just think of it: if a student was capable of testing a teacher, why would he need one. One cannot test a Guru. A Guru will make his presence felt through experiences.

- A formal education has no link with enlightenment and one's spiritual growth. Saint Kabir was illiterate yet his simple poetry on spiritualism is the resource for today's doctorate students.
- Embellishments are not worn by real Gurus. Donning a white robe or a long beard and matted hair does not make a man enlightened.
- A Guru is not one who learns scriptures by rote. Learning by rote is better done by a parrot.
- A Guru always remains in touch with his disciple; he first assesses him, chisels him and gives him all guidance at the right time.

❑❑❑

2

CHAPTER

Secrets of Breathing

What is the most important for a human being among money, fame and family? All these are important, yet the breath is indispensable for life and, therefore, tops the list. Just imagine a situation in which one's breath stops for 30 seconds. Ironically, we pay scant attention to our breath and are not inclined to understand or study it. For most of us, our body inhales and exhales air that we do feel and that is what breathing is all about. Many would wonder what more is there to learn about breathing. All actions and happenings in the life of humans–small or big–are linked to breathing. The process of breathing is intrinsically linked to all that happens to us–inside and outside the body.

Let's learn about the dynamics of breathing.

Why be Clueless about Breathing?

The reason why most of us do not care to study breathing is that it is one of the few involuntary tasks performed by our body. Breathing happens instinctively; we do not have to apply our mind or make an effort to do it.

God has not given us this responsibility. If it were so, then, maybe with our modern-day lifestyles, we would hear someone say, "Buddy, I was too busy to breathe; simply forgot!" Others may employ servants to breathe for him or outsource the vital life process!

Humans have an uncanny ability to improve their skills by first thinking about it and then practising the same to perfection. For example, our speech starts with blabbering and with each passing day, we continue practising it till we can speak properly. Similarly, we learn to walk, run, eat, and drink etc. by constantly working on our motor skills. As we are not required to think about performing the breathing, we do not even care.

Pay a little attention and you will realise that breathing is a dynamic activity. The constant changes it undergoes are its deep secrets. As we breathe effortlessly many readers might feel that knowing more about it is an 'unnecessary hassle'. The fact is that if one works on this 'unnecessary hassle' by learning the science of breathing, he can avoid many real 'hassles' in life.

Since the Vedic period, this land has given birth to specialists–Rishis and Munis–who contributed to making of Swara Gyan, the science of breathing and its secrets. Unfortunately, much of their work is either lost to the vagaries of time or exists in a distorted form today.

The antiquity and complexity of Sanskrit language is the key reason for this loss. Since all the ancient texts were written in Sanskrit that was spoken and read by the educated persons, many were lost over thousands of years. Those days, knowledge was kept as a secret treasure by the Gurus and imparted discreetly. This too led to the science of breathing going into oblivion and never appealed to the common man. Most of the texts available today are adulterated versions of the original ones. No wonder we remain clueless about the science of breathing.

However, the bits and pieces of authentic texts of Swara Gyan available today is an invaluable treasure trove of scientific knowledge. As we know, Science is not static; technologies and inventions overtake their earlier versions in no time. However, the fundamentals of any field of science remain unchanged.

Here, in this book, I would refer to the authentic facts of this science of breathing that have stood the test of the time. Each aspect of our life–health, business, friendship, sex, money, social relations, love and conflict–is linked to the breath of two people dealing with each other at a given time.

All things of the past, the present and the future have a connection with breathing. It is another thing that we are not conscious of it. Only if one becomes aware, he could change the situations of his life. The science of breathing is not a fantasy or an astrologer's prediction. The breath comprises myriad subtle reactions that can be easily decoded.

Swara Gyan is as scientific as Newton's Laws of motion. According to it, a person's success in a task is directly proportional to the compatibility of his breath at a given time. For instance, if you are breathing slowly and trying to get angry, it is impossible. For anger or sex to happen, you will automatically breathe fast. So, if one knows the secrets of breathing and practices, these can improve the quality of his life.

This wisdom was passed on to us from the times of Rishis and Munis, who had gained knowledge through a higher level of spiritual practices and experimentation. Those men and women sages were poles apart from today's ritual-promoting priests or purohits. The former studied a subject thoroughly and then used the knowledge gained through self-experimenting for drawing inferences. The positive results were disseminated to masses through stories, poems and essays. Unlike the modern-day priests and preachers, they didn't impose their knowledge on others. The modern priests feign their expertise by reciting the ancient texts learnt by rote. They do not use the information given in the texts for self-experimentation to experience the knowledge. For this reason, they fail to grasp the hidden meanings in these texts.

Probably it is for this reason that no new 'Shastra' (like Vedas, Geeta, Upanishads, Bible etc.) has been written for centuries. Humankind has not discovered new knowledge and, therefore, ancient texts remain irreplaceable and relevant. Since today's priests do not understand the hidden meanings in the ancient texts, they end up narrating a story. If someone from the audiences asks a critical question, they are likely to publically brand him as agnostic or atheist in order to silence him and discourage more questions. This is their way to camouflage their limited knowledge of Shastras.

They are not good at the interpolation of hidden meanings in these texts. These meanings can only be interpreted through Sadhna, a dedicated and hard regimen of self-experimentation.

Also, Swara Gyan can be learnt only through practice. Since dedicated and rigorous practice is not everyone's cup of tea, this science has remained out of the reach of the modern-day priests. The ancient sages had mastered the dynamics of Swara. For this reason, even today the basics of Swara Gyan remain unchanged. If you follow and practice it, you will get the same result as were discovered by pioneers of Swara Shastra, centuries ago.

Science of Breath

This is the oldest shastra of ancient Indian literature and nobody is sure of its origin. Lord Shiva had first revealed the secrets of breathing to his consort Parvati. Some readers would ask whether the chronicler of the Shiva-Parvati conversation was present as they discussed it. This question needs to be addressed, for nothing is unscientific and without logic in the shastra. In ancient times, the genre of conversational writing was popular.

For example, the text of a particular Kathopanishada is based on the conversation between Rishi Sanad and Narad, the bard of Devalok.

In those days, Rishis were not hungry for credit of their writings; their motivation was public good and compassion. They dedicated their books to the Gods and Goddess of learning. They would part with the knowledge they had painstakingly gathered for the benefit of future generations.

The loss of this heritage is tragic. Today, there are only a few experts of Swara Gyan. Some of them share this knowledge only with their close confidants while others have developed a vested interest in keeping it to themselves. The young learners, who are lucky to get this knowledge, also fail to practice it and therefore this legacy is in danger of not being passed on to the next generations.

This shloka, where Lord Shiva is telling Parvati the importance of the science of Swara, illustrates the complex writings in these texts:

Shloka (Shiva to Parvati)

स्वरज्ञानात्परं गुह्यम् स्वरज्ञनात्परं धनम्।
स्वरज्ञानत्परं ज्ञानं नवा दृष्टं नवा श्रुतम्॥

English Translation

No secret knowledge, bigger treasure or higher knowledge has ever been seen or heard of above the knowledge of 'Swara' (hidden subtle reactions happening during breathing).

The concept of hidden message in 'Shlokas' made the knowledge out of the realm of science and was eventually lost forever. Besides, the culture of applying the knowledge gained from the ancient texts was discontinued rendering the texts redundant.

Memorizing texts can never make one knowledgeable; if it were so, all those who can recite the holy books like Geeta, Bible and Quran would have seen God. Can one become a swimmer by reading books on swimming? He has to jump into a swimming pool, practice and learn the tricks from a coach. Otherwise, he would end up hurting himself.

As one cannot learn swimming without a coach, similarly, it is impossible to gain knowledge without a Guru. In the real-world we are surrounded by many charlatans masquerading as Gurus. This makes us think how can one find a Guru? Another ancient text Guru Geeta lays down rules for such a situation. It says one does not have to look for a Guru to guide him on the path of spirituality; it is the Guru who will eventually find his disciple. The reason is that a seeker should have a higher intellect and spiritual power to be able to judge his Guru. If such a person existed, then he surely could do without a Guru!

It is akin to the situation in which a student is searching for a good teacher. He is not qualified to choose one. Of course, he can seek recommendations from others. However, since the human experiences are also subjective even the perception and assessment of others can be misleading. Humans have developed a tendency to mistake opinion for a fact and knowledge. Knowledge cannot come without experience. A good Guru makes his disciple learn through his experiences and that alone is genuine knowledge.

Miracle

The Science of breathing is the only elevator that can lift us to the pinnacle of our spiritual journey. This must be seen in the context of what Shiva described to Parvati as Swara Gyan being the highest form of knowledge to have ever existed. In the modern world, few people believe that dhyana and Samadhi to be the real aims of human life. The majority of humans are in the pursuit of the mundane – food, house, clothing etc. They work hard to achieve material goals. Is it possible to make material gains by learning about the secrets of breathing? Can an understanding of this science make a difference to our daily routine?

The fact is one can improve the quality of his life by learning how to use the breath. This comes from daily practise. The pattern and chemistry of our breathing changes with different actions – eating, drinking, sleeping, walking, talking, resting, exercising, having sex, getting angry, spewing hate, showing compassion, being jealous etc. it is another matter that we are unaware of these changes since we never paid attention to the breath. If the change is compatible with a particular action, the result will be positive and if it is incompatible, the result will be adverse. Therefore, understanding the relationship between breathing and our actions will help us get the desired results in all our dealings in our daily life.

Breathing has a direct link with the mind and intellect. A thought first pops up in the mind, thereafter, we weigh its pros and cons and decide to either execute or abandon it. Our intellect – again controlled by breathing – supports us in it. Using our body parts, we execute the idea. This is Karma. As per the karmic theory, Karma is always rewarded. We would always want our karma to give us good results. Interestingly, while we wish so, we do not realise that the result of karma depends on the chemistry of breathing.

Experience It

It is not difficult to study the mysteries of breathing; and much easier to experience these and use the findings in our daily life. The universe is made of five elements. Everything including humans is also made of these elements. The five tatvas – the absolute truths that comprise the ultimate reality of creation we call God – Prithvi (earth), Aakash (sky), Vayu (air), Jal (water), and Agni (fire) – take turns to flow in our breath. After understanding this process, one can tweak his breathing to make it compatible with the task at his hands. By mastering this art, one can change adverse situations in one's life. One can even control the flow of a particular tatva to suit one's need at a given time. Learning the science of breathing is not time-consuming. Only in the initial stages, one needs to sit for long hours to practice and understand the concept. Later, one will always breathe consciously and effortlessly; it becomes an intrinsic part of one's system.

Whenever we face a failure, we do end up cursing our luck. Only if we knew about the impact, the tatva in our breath have on our actions, we would not do so. Humans being a small part of the Universe are also composed of the five elements.

For example, let's say Agni Tatva is flowing in one's breath and he gets angry. The person is liable to lose his cool though he may later repent his behaviour. In case Jal Tatva was flowing in his breath the time, his reaction would have been more appropriate.

When Vayu Tatva is flowing in one's breath, the person will not be able to concentrate on anything and feel helpless. If he's trying to read, his mind will not retain anything and he will end up saying, "I do not feel like studying".

Besides Tatva, the rhythm and pace of breathing are also important. For example, when one is angry or having sex, he would breathe fast. Performing these actions is impossible otherwise. Likewise, when the mind is peaceful, the breathing is either normal or very slow. That happens in Aakash Tatva. There is an intrinsic link between the state of our mind and the process of breathing. Slow breathing can calm our mind. So, we can change our breathing to feel calm. This is an oversimplified example. In the following chapters, you will learn in detail the secrets of breathing.

Law of Attraction & Breath

You might have heard about the 'Law of Attraction'. It works as precisely as the 'Law of Gravity'. Various spiritual Gurus and motivational speakers have spoken about this inherent law of the Universe. According to this principle one can attract positive or negative things into life through thoughts and actions.

Don't even think that it is just hearsay, because it is purely based upon scientific principles. Science says that the entire Universe is made up of energy, and obviously human beings are also a part of this energy. Therefore, the kind of energy you will create, it is bound to come back to you. We release energy through our emotions and thoughts. Meaning, your thoughts are greatly responsible for the things that manifest around you.

Some people feel that even if they are having positive thoughts, good things do not happen around them. So does it mean that this law doesn't work? No, the 'Law of Attraction' is always working.

So where is the problem? What really happens is that you can remember 10, 20 or even 100 times in a day to purposefully generate positive thoughts. But this is artificial, and the Law will not work. For that a strong willpower in our thoughts is a necessity. Only then will such thoughts arise continuously from within you, which you want. Now the question is how to generate such thoughts continuously in a natural manner?

Here lies the secret 'missing link' which is known to only a select few Siddha Gurus across the globe. That is your BREATH. Yes, the 'Secrets of Breath' are always working behind the 'Law of Attraction'. Without knowing these secrets, the Law cannot be fully understood.

Let us understand that Law of Attraction is directly related to our thinking, and all thoughts are generated in our mind. Mind is very subtle and its physical form is breath. Thereby it can be said that as will be the mind, so will be the breath and vice versa.

As mentioned earlier, by changing the rhythm of breath we can change the state of our mind. So obviously we can also govern our thoughts through breath.

Looking at it from Law of Attraction's point of view, you can control your thoughts by changing your breath and manifest anything each day, even every hour of your life.

This has been explained in detail in the following chapters.

You Can Change Your Life

By sitting daily for a couple of hours to practice the basics of breathing, one can experience the subtle reactions of the process. I can assure you that after practising for 10-15 days, you will experience its positive impact on life at your workplace, home or in a market. Intense and uninterrupted practice will make you an expert.

Through the book, I want to present the science of breathing from an ancient heritage for the benefit of the readers. To make it simple, I have decoded the Sanskrit hymns into simple ideas and doable actions.

Indians often refer to the ephemeral nature of life. We say each creature is born with limited breaths. However, nobody makes these limited breaths purposeful. Most of us do not even take a full breath and rather breathe shallowly. Despite knowing the oxygen in the air is vital for the body most of us do not inhale fully. It is only on the directions of a doctor we go for a walk in the park and inhale deep. Only a doctor makes us realise our folly. This complacency harms us. Because of our ignorance, we breathe in fast while we could do with slow breathing. This makes us consume our allotted breaths faster. The mantra to be kept in mind: Long life is linked to slow breathing.

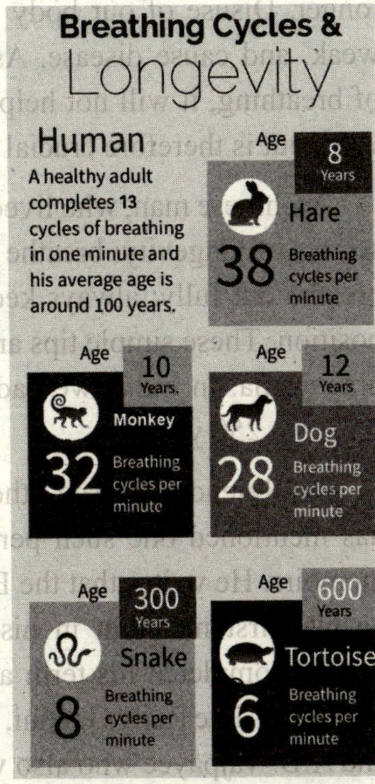

Secret of Longevity

A healthy adult completes 13 cycles of breathing in one minute and his average age is around 100 years. In comparison, a hare completes 38 cycles per minute and its average age is 8 years. Likewise, a monkey's breathing rate is 32 and it lives up to 10 years; a dog's cycle per minute is 28 and its average age 12 years. A snake lives 300 years with 8 breathing cycles per minute while a tortoise can live up to 600 years with just 6 breaths per minute!

During sexual activity, our breathing rises to 25-30 per minute. This is the reason why a person involved in this hard labour loses his body mass prematurely. It, however, does not mean that not doing physical work will keep one in pink of his health and he would live longer. Disuse of our body parts will make it stiff and weak, and cause disease. As disease increases the rate of breathing, it will not help us live longer. A moderate work out is therefore crucial for staying healthy.

A Chinese man, who lived for 165 years, revealed his secrets of longevity: breathe in deep up to the naval and breathe out fully; always keep your spine in an upright position. These simple tips are key elements of yoga and pranayama. In India, we had sages who lived in health for up to 250 years!

Dr Rajendra Prasad, the first President of India, has mentioned one such person, Devraha Baba, in his memoirs. He writes that the Baba looked the same when he had first met him in his childhood and later after he had completed his term as President in 1963. Other politicians like Rajiv Gandhi, V P Singh, Chandrashekhar and A.B. Vajpayee who also visited the Baba had passed away much before him. Devraha Baba died, in year 1990 at the age of 250 years.

What was the secret of Baba's longevity? I spoke with a journalist who had asked him this question. He had met him at Vrindavan, Uttar Pradesh. As he asked the sage replied, "Oh Son! It's not such a big deal; ask me about something else". However, when he insisted, the Baba said, "Run moon in the day and sun in the night; it can make one a Yogi".

Devraha Baba

His reply didn't make sense to the news-driven journalist and he was rather disappointed. The Baba had answered honestly while the visitor had failed to make sense of it.

The meaning of Baba's words dawned on me many years later, after my Guru had asked me to focus on breathing. Only after years of practice, I understood the meaning of 'moon and sun' referred to by Devraha Baba.

The sun and the moon have a strong connection with our breathing. This link is synchronised perfectly and is precise up to a split second. The breathing works in tandem with the movement of the sun and moon. This process is, however, interrupted by our unnatural routine. We can, however, change this.

RECAP

- Pay attention to your breath to feel how it is constantly changing. The changes incorporate secrets.
- The secret elements of our breath control all events of our life in the past, present and the future.
- Five Tatvas – Prithvi (Earth), Jal (water), Vayu (air), Agni (fire), Aakash (sky) – flow in our breath one by one.
- Breathing can help us gain anything: material possessions, sex life, spiritual growth and literally everything.
- The slower the rate of breathing the longer a creature lives. In the absence of this knowledge, we often end up breathing fast when it is not needed.

❑❑❑

3

CHAPTER

What is the Science of Swara?

Before we study the Science of Swara, it's important to understand the difference between breath and Praan. In India when a person dies, we say, "he has left his body, or Praan has left his body". Praan is linked to life and therefore breathing is linked with Praan. Modern science is yet to find if the air we breathe has elements like Praan in it. However, researchers have found secret elements in the breath.

Renowned German doctor and psychologist Dr. Wilhelm Reich says in his research paper, "We don't just breathe air; the air is the base of breath but it has a secret element. This is not a physical one like the air. The breath carries an invisible element". He called it Orgone energy. This can also be called vital energy. It's life energy.

This means that breathing involves more than just air. In ancient Indian texts, this element is called Praan. We can call it divine energy flowing through the air. Praan can also be likened to air for its omnipresence; it can be experienced and felt. For example, when one visits a sick person in a hospital, he experiences an inner loss as if something has been sucked from inside him.

This is because a sick person needs more Praan energy to live, and he absorbs it from his surroundings. For the same reason, one feels tired after a visit to the hospital. Likewise, moving in a crowded place one feels claustrophobic; others are sapping one's energy. This feeling of loss of energy doesn't happen when one is alone; on the other hand, one feels peacefulness.

Similarly, when you meet an energetic person, you experience a gush of energy inside you. Also, people who like each other, like men and women, are constantly exchanging the Praan energy. The interflow of Praan energy is the reason behind their mutual attraction. On the other hand, meeting a person with negative energy makes one feel suffocated, peevish and angry.

Reiki is a Japanese system of healing through Praan energy. In India, people have been experimenting with Praan energy since times immemorial. Take for example Pranayama that is made of "Praan" and "Ayaam" (dimension). The word means linking one's life energy (Praan) to another dimension (of creation) and also the other way round–linking the new dimension to one's Praan.

In Indian tradition, one touches the feet of one's parents or Guru to seek their blessings. This is another example of receiving positive energy as energy flows from fingers and toes. When one touches the feet of an elder with a sense of devotion, a part of his energy flows to the blessing-seeker. The other part of energy flows when the elderly person puts his hand on the head of the seeker. This completes the circuit of energy.

For this reason, a Siddha Guru (a person who has reached a higher level of spirituality) doesn't allow people to touch his feet. If the seeker somehow manages to do that, he refrains from touching his head with his hand; he will raise his hand in the air to bless him. It's not that he does't want to part with their energy, the real reason is that he realises that his energy level and quality cannot be handled by the seeker. For this reason, he blesses him with a gesture – raising of hand in air with his palm in the direction of the seeker.

Devraha Baba, whose story is written in detail in the second chapter of the book, never touched anyone's head for blessings. He lived in a tree house, a few feet above the ground where people visited him for blessings and darshan. Only if he felt like, he would touch the head of the blessing-seeker with his feet hung in the air. People, including Prime Ministers, would clamour for a touch of his feet and yet just a few were privileged to get it.

This explains the logic behind the Indian custom of youngsters touching the feet of their parents and Gurus. Some even do it by bowing their head at their feet.

Indian spiritual practitioners have done thousands of experiments in Praan energy. However, modern science is yet to delve into this area. Since Science doesn't believe without exploring all facets, this remains an unexplored area.

Nevertheless, it doesn't mean that Praan is nothing more than the air we breathe; it only means that modern science is yet to explore beyond Dr. Wilhelm Reich's findings. This is a pending project of modern science.

The above explanation is to make the readers understand that in the Science of Swara, breathing means Praan energy.

The passage through which Praan Vayu (vital energy) reaches each cell of the human body and comes out is called 'Nadi'. According to the ancient Literature of Swara, a human body has 7200 Nadis. A Nadi has no physical form like a capillary or nerve; it is a route for movement of Praan Vayu inside our body and therefore, cannot be detected with an X-ray machine or by physiological examination.

In ancient texts, Lord Shiva speaks to Parvati about Nadi as follows:

Shloka (Shiva to Parvati)

देहमध्ये स्थिता नाड्यो बहुरूपाः सुविस्तरात्।
ज्ञातव्याश्च बुधैर्नित्यं स्वदेहज्ञानहेतवे॥

English Translation

A human body has a vast network of Nadi. The wise men must gain knowledge about the network of Nadi in the human body.

The Nadi system originates at the navel and fans out across the body symmetrically. The system contains the latent divine energy called Kundalini. A set of ten Nadis each branch out from the navel point towards the upper and the lower part of the body. Besides a set of two Nadis each branch out diagonally up and down from the same point. That makes up for 24 Nadis. Of these, ten are the most important ones and each one carries a different Pran Vayu to enable the body to perform different functions.

At the intersection of Nadis, Chakras are formed. (Chakras will be dealt with exclusively in another chapter). Of the 24 key Nadis, ten are vital for survival. These are: (1) Ida, (2) Pingla, (3) Sushumna. (4) Gandhari, (5) Hastijivha, (6) Poosha, (7) Yashaswini, (8) Alambusha, (8) Kuhu and (10) Shankhini.

Ida is located in the left and Pingla on the right side of the spine while Sushumna is in the middle part; Gandhari is in the left and Hastijivha in the right eye;

Poosha in the right ear and Yashaswini in the left; Alambusha in the mouth, Kuhu in the genitals and Shankhini in the rectum.

However, of these, Ida, Pingla and Sushumna are the most important Nadis and are located in the Pran Marga (passage of life). Their study is most crucial for gaining knowledge of Swara Shastra.

Readers must keep in mind that Ida Nadi is also called 'Chandra Nadi' after Moon and its disposition is feminine. Pingla called the 'Surya Nadi' after Sun, has masculine disposition. Ida's dominant trait is feminine while Pingla's is masculine.

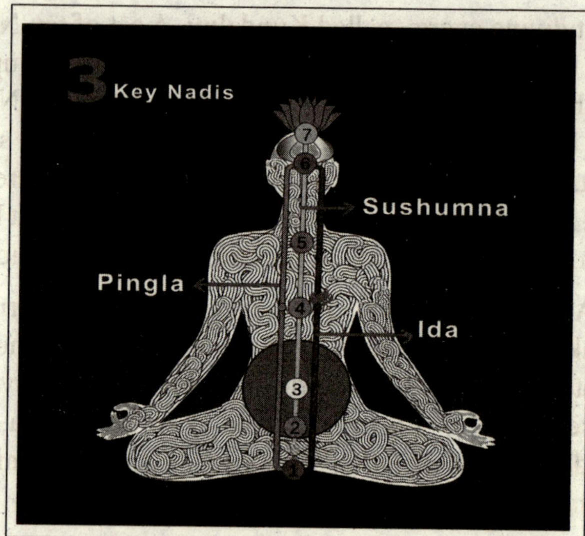

Unless we learn about the secrets of the three key Nadis, it is beyond one's imagination to think that everything in the world can be changed with the help of Nadis. Shiva Swara Shastra is dedicated to this particular science. Generally, we believe that a Sanskrit text is always about religion. That's a baseless assumption. Swara Shastra even explains how to improve the man-woman relationship and produce a 'designer' baby. The Shastra deals with all that humans are into.

The following shlokas illustrate this point:

Shloka (Shiva to Parvati)

शत्रून्हन्यात् स्वबले तथा मित्र समागमः।
लक्ष्मीप्राप्तिः स्वरबले कीर्तिः स्वरबले सुखम्॥

English Translation

The power of Swara can defeat the enemy; bring together estranged friends, shower blessings of Mother Durga and bounties of fame and prosperity and everything else.

Shloka (Shiva to Parvati)

कन्याप्राप्ति स्वरबले स्वरतो राजदर्शनम्।
स्वरेण देवतासिद्धिः स्वरेण क्षितिपो वशः॥

English Translation

The knowledge of Swara can make one meet his soul mate; get an audience with the King, the blessings of Devtas and a positive message from the King (ruler).

The following shlokas make it clear that higher knowledge is not only helpful in acquiring material success; it can also lead one on the spiritual path of self-realisation. The science of Swara contains secrets of success in both the physical and spiritual world. It is, therefore, regarded as the best source of spiritual knowledge. Look at the following shloka:

Shloka (Shiva to Parvati)

सर्वशास्त्रपुराणादि स्मृतिवेदांगपूर्वकम्।
स्वरज्ञानात्परं तत्त्वं नास्ति किंचिद्वरानने॥

English Translation

The knowledge of Swara is the greatest of all Shastras like Vedas, Pranas, etc.

Shloka (Shiva to Parvati)

इदं स्वरोदयं शास्त्रं सर्वशास्त्रोत्तमोत्तमम्।
आत्मघट प्रकाशार्थ प्रदीपकलिकोपमम्॥

English Translation

(Shiva addressing Parvati) The knowledge of Swara is the greatest of all; it illuminates us from inside with the glow of knowledge.

It is surprising that for its entire scientific basis, this treasure trove of knowledge has remained in oblivion. There could be two reasons for it. One: the practitioners of Swara Gyan of those days must have preserved it with the intention to save it from falling into the wrong hands. The other could be the self-interests of those who knew its importance; probably, they didn't want to share it with others. Since Shiva begins by telling Parvati that this knowledge should be imparted only to select ones and not to all and sundry, the first reason seems more plausible.

Here are a few more relevant shlokas;

Shloka (Shiva to Parvati)

शांते शुद्धे सदाचारे गुरुभक्त्यैकमानसे।
दृढ़चित्ते कृतज्ञे च देयं चैव स्वरोदयम्॥

दुष्टे च दुर्जने क्रुद्धे नास्तिके गुरुतल्पगे।
हीनसत्त्वेदुराचारे स्वरज्ञानं न दीयते॥

English Translation

Hey Parvati, only a person who is calm and well behaved;

has a pure Chitta (consciousness); is devoted to his Guru (master) and determined is the right one to inherit this knowledge.

A cruel man, a non-believer, epicurean, untruthful and has many vices should never be imparted this knowledge.

These shlokas allude to the worries of the creator of Swara Gyan about these scriptures falling in the wrong hands. He was keen to keep it a secret and reveal it to only worthy men. Maybe for this reason, in the opening chapters of Swara Shastra its secrecy has been emphasized repeatedly. It seems the writer wanted to share this knowledge by writing it down but was cautious about its misuse or wrong interpretation. This may be the reason why the writer has consciously written in a way that it is too complex to understand.

A fantastic trick has been used for this: the shlokas are dispersed over different pages. For example, a shloka of 20 lines is split thus – the first line on page 5, next on page 9, and the third one on 187. Just imagine how complicated it is made deliberately. Only a student with a keen desire to acquire knowledge can figure it out. A casual reader will fail to pursue it as it would make no sense to him. The idea to deliberately and yet purposefully create a complicated text is a great idea.

The complexity of Shiva Swara Shastra is also because of Sanskrit that gradually became a redundant language. Like all ancient texts, this one is also written in Sanskrit, read and spoken by only a select elite group of the learned men. Gradually, Sanskrit was being used by fewer people and reached the brink of extinction.

Besides, the rules of Sanskrit grammar have also changed drastically making its comprehension difficult for the generations that came after its creation. Apparently in this Shastra, the easy and scientific thoughts given in 364 shlokas are presented in a highly complicated manner making most readers give up as soon as they begin.

Others treat the Shastra as divine and show reverence towards it. However, the readers would get a pithy version of all the wisdom contained in the ancient text.

Though Shiva Swara Shastra never became popular yet sadhus with higher spiritual powers do the Swara Sadhna as their fundamental practice. They usually settle down in a quiet place for Sadhna making everyone wonder about their activities.

Devraha Baba who lived up to 250 years was a practitioner of Swara Shastra. While revealing the secret of his long years to my journalist friend, he had referred to 'running of sun and moon'. In fact, later only I realised he was referring to Ida (moon) and Pingla (sun) Nadis! Sun and Moon have a direct impact on our body through these two Nadis. In the upcoming chapters, we will study more about this phenomenon.

At a given time our one nostril is majorly involved in breathing. The other one gets active after an hour. When we are breathing through the right nostril, it means, our Pingla Nadi is active. When the left one is in use, it is about the Ida Nadi. In between, for a brief period of four minutes, breathing happens through both the nostrils. At this stage, our Sushumna Nadi is at work. Sushumna is also called Sandhikaal (sandhi means union and kaal means time); it is the union of the two other key Nadis.

According to Swara Shastra, the air we breathe through nostril is Prana, the vital energy. The breath is called Swara. Breathing is a highly organized activity in our body. Basic knowledge about it can help improve our lives. One is not required to use complex scientific formulae, rules of mathematics, meditate for years and perform bizarre rituals to acquire this knowledge. It is quite easy and anyone can practice it. A sustained practise of following the pace and direction of the breath will make you enjoy the benefits of this knowledge all your life.

Human beings cannot always multitask. For example, running and eating at thc same time is difficult while driving your car and speaking on the mobile phone can be easily done. However, we cannot talk on the phone while learning how to drive.

Likewise, while starting the study of Swara Shastra, one has to maintain the focus. Only after due practice, one can do normal work along regulating the breath. Gradually and through sustained practice, the knowledge about breathing gets into your subconscious mind; it remains on as you do routine chores and perform responsibilities. However, one has to be careful about the compatibility of the job at hand with the Nadi.

The compatibility is important since it will determine the outcome-success and failure. In Swara Shastra, these two states of Swara are referred to as 'good omen' (Shubha) and 'bad omen' (Ashubha). The moot point is we can control the Nadi.

In the following chapters, I will discuss in detail the compatibility of Nadi with different jobs that human have to do.

RECAP

- A human body has 7200 Nadis of which three are the most important.
- These are: Ida, Pingla and Sushumna. Understanding of these three can give us better control over our life.
- During breathing, our body uses one nostril at a time.
- It changes after an hour. Both nostrils take turns for breathing at the gap of one hour.
- When the left nostril is functioning, it means Ida Nadi is active, and when the right nostril is breathing, it is the turn of Pingla. After each hour it changes and before the changeover, both the nostrils get active simultaneously for approximately four minutes, thereby, invoking Sushumna Nadi.

- Ida is linked to the Moon and Pingla to the Sun; both celestial bodies have a direct impact on our body.

- One can do normal work while practising the art of breathing. The only care one must take is there should be compatibility between the work at hand and the Nadi at a given time.

- You can easily change the Nadi to suit your purpose.

❑❑❑

4

CHAPTER

How to Feel Nadi?

It's easy to identify the active Nadi at a given time. It involves doing a simple exercise: close your eyes and focus on the air being exhaled. You will soon realise that the exhalation is majorly happening through one nostril. If your left nostril is doing that, it means your Ida Nadi is active; in the case of the right nostril, it is Pingla. After some time, you may feel that both the nostrils are equally involved in exhalation. At this stage, it is your Sushumna Nadi. This stage of breathing is also called Shunya Swara (Shunya in Sanskrit means zero, blank or space). Pingla's masculine traits link it to the Sun and Ida's femininity is influenced by the Moon. Sushumna is located right in the middle of the spine while Ida is located on the left and Pingla on the right.

Follow this method to identify the active Nadi:

1. Sit with a calm mind and focus on breathing. Take your index finger close to your nostrils and exhale. You will feel that the air from one nostril is particularly strong. The Nadi on that side is active at that time.

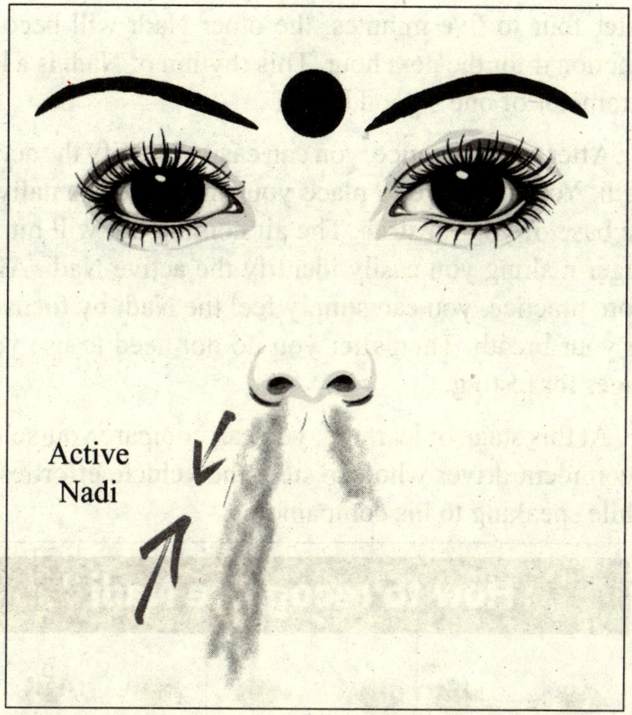

2. Block one nostril by pressing your finger against it and breathe in from the other. Repeat this with the other one. You will realise that breathing is easier from only one nostril. The Nadi on that side is active at that time.

It is important to keep in mind that after each hour the other Nadi will become active. However, in between the switchover, for a period of four to five minutes, you will notice that both the nostrils are breathing with the same force. At this stage, your Sushumna Nadi is active.

After four to five minutes, the other Nadi will become functional for the next hour. This rhythm of Nadi is a key parameter of one's good health.

After some practice, you can easily identify the active Nadi. You just have to place your finger horizontally at the base of your nostrils. The air coming out will hit the finger making you easily identify the active Nadi. After more practice, you can simply feel the Nadi by focusing on your breath. Thereafter you do not need to use your finger for testing.

At this stage of learning, you can compare yourself to a confident driver who can steer the vehicle effortlessly while speaking to his companion.

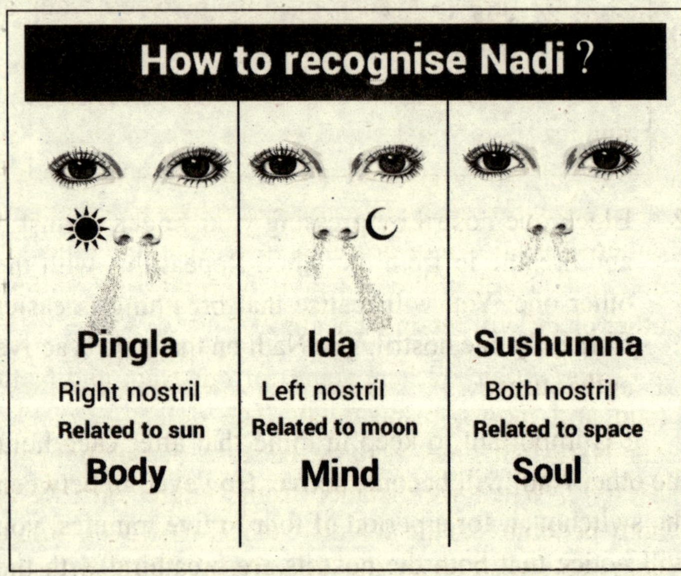

You must know that your Nadi is perfectly synchronised with Nature, especially sun and moon. As the sunrise and sunset occur at the precise time in Nature, Ida, Pingla and Sushumna take turns to get activate at a precise time and in a cyclic fashion. The switchovers happen at regular intervals and the process is as precise as the time. At the time of the birth of a human being, his Nadi is in perfect harmony with the sun and moon.

As we grow, our unnatural routine, unhealthy food habits, wired sleep cycle etc. have an impact on our Nadi. After defying nature and adopting an unscientific lifestyle, we start moving away from Nature. This is the beginning of misery and problems of all kinds in our lives. This throws synchronisation between Nadi and Nature to the wind.

This can be understood with a simple example: A person has two clocks and he has synchronised their needles to split second precision so that both show the same time. Suddenly, one clock develops a defect and it either slows down or becomes faster than the other. The defective watch will never give the right time while the other clock will retain its accuracy.

The two clocks here stand for our Nadi and Nature (sun and moon) respectively. The defective clock is our Nadi that goes haywire because of our unhealthy lifestyle. When we distance from Nature, our life and body become like the defective clock. However, with the help of Swara Vigyan, the defective clock (Nadi) can be cured back to health.

A healthy human body has a fixed temperature which is maintained by Ida, Pingla and Sushumna. Ida is influenced by Moon and has a cooling impact; Pingla by Sun and it generates warmth in the body. Sushumna is influenced by the sky that regulates temperature at a particular level in the body. This system can be compared with the working of an air conditioner. The thermostat of an air conditioner works till the temperature reaches the desired level before switching off. The three Nadis also work in the same manner to maintain the optimum temperature in the human body.

In the initial days of the birth of a human being, his Nadi is somewhat erratic. However, on the first day of the waning moon fortnight, exactly at sunrise, the child's Pingla gets activated. This starts the rhythmic cycle of Nadi. Likewise, if the first day of the waxing moon fortnight comes earlier, at sunrise, his Ida Nadi becomes active. As soon as the child's body imbibes heat from Nature, his Ida is activated as it lowers the temperature. Likewise, Pingla gets activated as soon as the body needs to increase the temperature in the next fortnight.

The cyclic switchover between the two is synchronised in a manner that automatically at the moon rise it will be the turn of Pingla. This cycle continues 24×7 in our body, uninterrupted.

An infant's behaviour is directly linked to his Nadi system. When the child cries for food, defecates or gets angry, we should know that his Pingla is active; when he urinates his Ida is at work. In the Sushumna mode, the child smiles a lot, feels happy and even falls asleep.

Unfortunately, this natural process that links the human body to Nature is unwittingly interrupted by the child's parents. Humans are the only species that tend to wean their newborn from Nature. Another interesting fact is that it is only the humans who are blessed with the system of Nadi, and that makes us superior species. It is pathetic that we tend to live in abject ignorance of this great attribute and end up distancing ourselves from Nature.

The child only expresses through crying. His parents and other elders at home often tend to attribute his crying to a few known reasons: hunger pangs, sleepiness, need for changing nappy or stomach ache etc. Everyone gets into a frenzy to either make him sleep or feed him, even forcibly. They do not realise that the child is crying perhaps because his Pingla Nadi has run its hour and now Ida has just got active. At this stage, the mother feeds him out of sheer love and concern. What happens to his Nadi? Pingla would have to get activated so that the body can digest the food. Feeding interrupts the natural cycle and interferes with his body's rhythm.

Gradually, the natural Nadi cycle of our body starts facing impediments; the activity of breathing that should be in sync with Nature goes for a toss. Apart from feeding the child when he does not need food, making him sleep on the side of the active Nadi would lead to the sudden activation of the Nadi on the opposite side in five minutes. The rule is if you lay on the right side of your body, your Pingla gets activated and if on the right, the Ida steps in.

As most of us have no idea of the Nadi system, a mother simply puts her child to sleep on either side of his body. From this begins the process of destabilisation of the equation between the body and Nature. With such parental care', the Nadi system in a grown-up goes completely haywire; the coordination between Nature and the cycles of Nadis out of control.

However, let me clarify, if by changing the side while sleeping, the Nadi is interrupted, it would eventually return to normal at the sunrise. However, if the Nadi has to change because a child has been fed at the wrong time, it does not readjust to natural rhythm. Since we have no idea about it, this continues and upsetting our other body functions too.

We never get to realise that it is harmful to eat while Ida is active; to go for urination when Pingla is active. With this not only our bodies become sick we also end up botching our routine activities.

In Indians homes, elders often ask young children to lie down on the left side after a meal. The logic behind it is that while sleeping on the left side, Pingla gets activated and that stimulates digestion. Not following this sleeping on the right and invoking Ida – leads to indigestion, constipation and general unease of the gut.

Traditional Hindus who wear the holy thread, Janeoo, are supposed to lift and wrap it over their earlobe while urinating. Today most men follow this as a ritual without knowing that its real purpose is to press a point behind the ear that activates Ida. This takes care of the health of kidneys and maintaining libido.

All this may look too complex to follow. Like should one wait for Ida Nadi to get active for going to the washroom? What if someone needs to urinate urgently? Those who have knowledge of Nadi have given tips to make quick corrections in our system. Like if one needs to urinate and his Pingla is active, by pressing a particular point in the ear region, he can quickly make his Ida active.

Course Correction

To understand the method for the course correction of our Nadi system one must know about the Hindi calendar or Panchang. It is a lunar calendar comprising two fortnights called the Paksha (sides). One Paksha is when the moon waxes and the other when it wanes. The waxing period called Shuklpaksha ends with a full moon day – Purnima or Puranmashi. The next fortnight, called the Krishna Paksha (dark side) starts with a full moon and advances towards the no moon night. Each day has a specific name and the Paksha ends either with Puran Mashi (full moon) or Amavasya (no moon). Pratipada is the name of the first day of each Paksha.

A healthy body will have Ida functioning at the time of sunrise on Shuklpaksha Pratipada (first day of waxing moon fortnight) while at the same time on the Pratipada of Krishan Paksha, Pingla should be active. This sequence continues for three days. On the fourth day, at sunrise, there will be a changeover of Nadis. This time, Pingla would be active. In a way, the Nadi change at sunrise happens after three days. This sequence continues for a Paksha leading to activation of Pingla on the first day of Krishna Paksha at sunrise.

Another rule of Nature is: the opposite Nadis will be active at the time of sunrise and moonrise each day. On a day when at sunrise, Ida is active, it would be automatically the turn of Pingla at moonrise the same day.

The life of a person who becomes aware of the Nadi system is sure to be beautiful and full of possibilities. He will realise that his Pingla is active when he feels hungry and Ida when he feels like urinating.

After practising it for a few months, a person's Nadi system gets synchronised with Nature. The mantra is: if the right side Nadi is active at sunrise your body will remain in harmony with nature throughout the day.

You do not have to wait for pratipada to start to harmonize your body with nature:

Follow the chart below to start the first cycle at the time of sunrise:

Krishna Paksha day

1,2,3 Pingla

4,5,6 Ida

7,8,9 Pingla

10, 11,12 Ida

13,14,15 Pingla

At sunrise on the day one of Shukla Paksha, it will be the turn of Ida and the sequence will continue. We can use the above chart to detect the active Nadi at sunrise on any day and accordingly, make corrections.

How to Change Nadi?

Changing the Nadi is quite easy. On a given day (see the above chart) you wake up ten minutes before the sunrise and check the active Nadi. This should be done while you are still in bed. If the right Nadi is active (as per the chart) you can lie down on the opposite side. For example, for activating Pingla lie down on the left side and for Ida on the right. This is the way to ensure that at the exact time of sunrise, the requisite Nadi is active. In case you need to change the Nadi, lie down on the side of the active Nadi. You will get the desired result.

In fact, you can change Nadi in any position – standing, walking or sitting. One way is to press your armpit with a tight fist on the side of the active Nadi for a few minutes. The other trick is to close your nostril that is majorly involved in breathing with your thumb or any object and take a deep breath from the other. Hold your breath as long as possible and then release it from the same side. Repeat it five to ten times and you will find that your Nadi has changed.

It is amazing to know that this calculation about the Nadi cycle dates to an era when there were no clocks. Those people used a different system of calculating time.

A healthy human body should have Ida and Pingla working alternatively for one hour. In case, either or both fall short or exceed the time limit, the body is unhealthy. Such a body requires course correction to get back into health.

Besides sun and moon, our Nadi system is also affected by other celestial bodies. As we know, the rotating planets impact the earth and entire nature; since our body is part of Nature, it also faces changes due to this phenomenon.

The Sun has the greatest impact on life on Earth. The next is the moon, a star that is closest to Earth. On the full moon night (Puranmashi) the high tide phenomenon is the scientific explanation of the impact of the moon on oceans. Since our body's 80 per cent part is water, the same force of the Moon applies to it as well.

Interestingly, the water in our body and the sea has the same ratio of salinity.

Many studies have pointed that most suicides happen on Puranmashi, the full moon night. On this day, the gravitational pull of the moon is at its peak and it impacts our thoughts and disposition of the human mind. Moon enhances one's state of mind – a happy person becomes happier and a sad one becomes sadder, or even depressed.

RECAP

- Identifying a Nadi is an easy and simple process. Check the flow of air coming out of the nostrils.

If the outflow is forceful from the right side, Pingla Nadi is active; if it is from the left one, then Ida is at work. When both nostrils are exhaling at the same rate, the Sushumna Nadi is at work. This is also called Shunya (zero) Swara.

- Pingla is masculine while Ida is feminine in character. The Nadi of a new-born is in perfect harmony with Nature.
- Wrong habits and lack of healthy routine plays havoc with our Nadi system; it becomes erratic.
- We can easily re-align our Nadi system with Nature to lead a life full of health and happiness.

❑❑❑

5

CHAPTER

Flow of Tatva in Our Body

The Human body is made of five Tatvas (elements): Prithvi (Earth), Jal (water), Agni (Fire), Vayu (Air) and Aakash (Space). The Tatva flow one by one in Ida and Pingla and identifying them is not so diffcult. However, one should not try to rush through. For the initial four days, try to feel the Nadi – Ida and Pingla. Only after that one should start practice of Tatva.

As our body is made up of five Tatva, Hindus described the death as the process of one's merger with Five Tatva.

After death, a human body is disposed of through cremation, burial or laid at rest in a river. In all these, elements of the body merge into the soil (Prithvi); evaporate as water (Jal) or as gas or steam into the air (Vayu). The Agni of the body merges with heat in the atmosphere – the heat of the soil in case of burial, in the atmosphere in case of cremation. The remaining Akash Tatva of the body blends with space.

Space is not insignificant; in fact, it is the most important part of the creation.

Here is an explanation:

We raise walls and fix doors and windows to build a house. The house is actually the space between the walls and not the walls, doors, windows and other fixtures.

This analogy illustrates the importance of space. If there was no space, there would be no sound. As it is said that the most important things in life come in small packets, Akash Tatva surfaces in the Nadi for the least time.

At the time of the switch over between Ida and Pingla, for the first four minutes, the Akash Tatva flows. It is followed by Vayu for 8 minutes, Agni for 12 minutes, Jal for 16 minutes and Prithvi for the remaining 20 minutes, in that order. After an hour, the Nadi changes and Tatva flow in the same order in the other Nadi.

How can one recognise and assess the impact of the Tatva on the body? Let's begin with an understanding that all things or objects that we see around are identified only in five ways: through looks, taste, smell, texture (touch) and sound. These properties are called five Tanmatra. The five Tanmatras are experienced through our five senses – tongue, eyes, ear, skin and nose. Since human being acquires knowledge through the five senses, they can do so the same with Tatva.

Ancient texts like Vedas, Upanishads and Swara Gyan describe Panchtatva Gyan (Knowledge of Tatva) as the highest form of knowledge. One who gets through to it need not explore more horizons. For this, we need to understand the meaning of the following Shlokas, part of a conversation between Lord Shiva and Parvati:

Shloka (Parvati to Shiva)

देवदेव महादेव कृपां कृत्वा ममोपरि।
सर्वसिद्धिकरं ज्ञानं वदयस्व मम प्रभो॥
कथं ब्रह्माण्डमुत्पन्नं कथं वा परिवर्त्तते।
कथं विलीयते देव वद ब्रह्माण्डनिर्णयम्॥

English Translation

Oh Lord, kindly tell me about the ultimate knowledge to reach the absolute truth. How was the universe created? What is behind its dynamic nature? How does it end into?

Shloka (Shiva to Parvati)

तत्त्वाद् ब्रह्माण्डमुत्पन्नं तत्त्वेन परिवर्त्तते।
तत्त्वेविलीयते देवि तत्त्वाद् ब्रह्माण्डनिर्णयः॥

English Translation

The Universe originates from Tatva; it changes due to Tatva and at the end merges with it. Tatva is the Root of the Universe. Likewise, the cycle of creation, its destruction and rejuvenation goes on.

Shloka (Parvati asks, again:)

तत्त्वमेव परं मूलं निश्चितं तत्त्ववादिभिः।
तत्त्वस्वरूपं किं देव तत्त्वमेव प्रकाशय॥

English Translation

How come Tatva is the cause of creation, its existence, destruction and end? What are these Tatva?

(Shiva gives a detailed reply in the following four shlokas)

निरंजनो निराकार एको देवो महेश्वरः ।
तस्मादाकाशमुत्पन्नमाकाशाद्वायुसंभवः ॥
वायोस्तेजस्ततश्चापस्ततः पृथ्वीसमुद्भवः ।
एतानि पंचतत्त्वानि विस्तीर्णानि पंचधा ॥
तेभ्यो ब्रह्माण्डमुत्पन्नं तैरेव परिवर्त्तते ।
विलीयते च तत्रैव तत्रैव रमते पुनः ॥
पंचतत्त्वमये देहे पंचतत्त्वानि सुन्दरि ।
सूक्ष्म रूपेण वर्त्तन्ते ज्ञायन्ते तत्त्वयोगिभिः ॥

English Translation

The creation owes its origins to Lord Maharashtra (Shiva), the unborn and the formless. From him rose Aakash (space), and from it emerged the Vayu(air); the Vayu gave rise to Agni (fire) and from the latter rose Jal (water). The water in turn, created Prithvi (earth).

Together these five Tatva formed Srishti, the creation. As the Tatva created the Universe, this would also cause its merger with the Tatva at the end. The cycle of creation will continue till infinity.

Likewise, the human body is also built of these Tatva; these exist in a subtle form in the body and affect changes inside.

Only the Tatvayogi (Yogis who do the Sadhna of Tatva) know everything about these. Tatvayogis can unravel the secrets of Tatva and see the inner light.

This means that the complete experience of Tatva is possible only when one reaches the pinnacle of spirituality. I will deal with spiritualism later as this chapter is confined to understanding the impact of Nadi on our life and identification of Tatva. Each Tatva has a distinct smell, colour, taste, texture and sound.

Swami Paramhans Satyananda was the first to enumerate the method of recognising Tatva through Dhyana. According to him, one could acquire knowledge of Tatvas through Dhyana in Shanmukhi mudra (a yoga posture). In this posture, one has to use his thumbs as earplugs, middle fingers to block the nostrils, ring and little fingers to block the mouth and close his eyes with index fingers. (There is mention of Chakra in the following text. The Chakra will be dealt with in detail in the coming chapter).

Close your eyes and open the mouth as if you want to make the sound of whistling. This is called Kaki Mudra. Breathe from the mouth and feel that the Prana (vital energy) is rising from Muladhara Chakra upwards to Agya Chakra. While breathing, focus your mind on Muladhara Chakra. As you breathe in, you will feel a sensation, the energy oozing and rising up. By the time you complete the breathing, this energy blob will reach Agaya Chakra, located in the middle of brows.

As you feel the blob of energy touching Agya Chakra, hold your breath as long as possible.

Maintain your Kaki Mudra pose; curl your tongue to touch the roof of the mouth and bend your head without touching the neck in the Jalandhar bandha pose. In this process, you have to maintain focus on the blob of energy at Agya Chakra.

Straighten up your head and exhale normally through nostrils. Repeat this sequence of breathing five times and take a break after each round with eyes closed. After this exercise, sit silently in a peaceful place. With eyes closed, look into the emptiness, called Chidakaash. Soon a colour will emerge on this blank image denoting the Tatva flowing in the Nadi. Yellow colour denotes Prithvi; white stands for Jal; red for Agni; blue or brown for Vayu, black or mixed colours for Aakash. One should ignore the initial images since the real one will come at the end.

Length of Breath

Take your hands close to your nostrils as you exhale. As the breath hits your hand, slowly move the hand away till the breath no longer touches it. Measure this length with the width of your fingers or thread. The relation between the length and each Tavta will be discussed further.

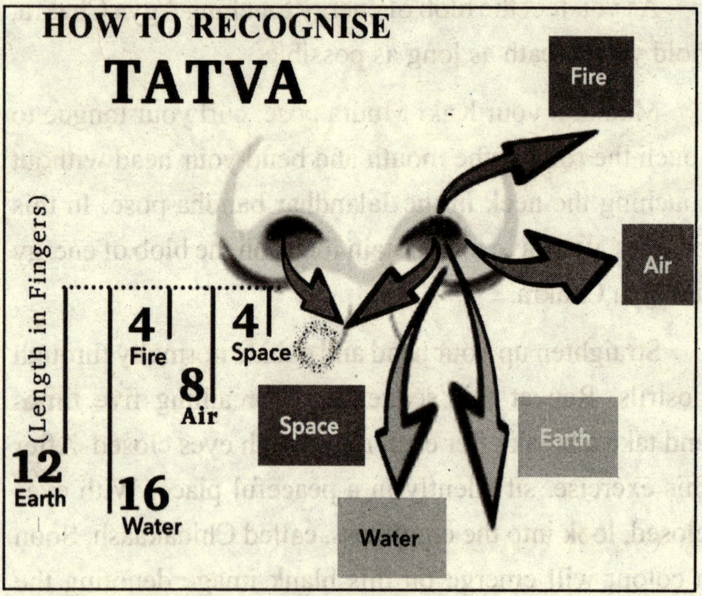

Tatva Through Touch

Close your eyes and focus on your breath. Feel the areas of the nostril that the air touches before being expelled. It either moves as a swirl touching all sides of the nostril; diagonally touching the side of the nostril that's closer to the ear; or it moves straight, touching the skin above lips. Each specific direction alludes to the Tatva. Besides, a person with a healthy body can easily identify the Tatva by studying the direction or the length of his outflowing breath and some other ways (to be studied later) by simple awareness.

Flow of Tatva in Our Body

Aakash (Space) Tatva

When Aakash Tatva is flowing, Ida and Pingla work in tandem. At this stage, you may feel confused about the Nadi. Sometimes it is Ida and the other time you feel it is Pingla; in between both the nostrils seem to be equally involved in breathing. The breath is very short – just 4 finger long – and can only be felt by taking hand very close to the nose. In this stage, the breath has a normal temperature and it moves inside the nostril in a swirl.

Akash Tatva stays for 4 minutes. In this phase, Dhyana and praying are highly recommended. No success can be achieved in any other task. Akash Tatva is the cause of hate, jealousy, fear, shyness and infatuation.

In Dhyana, this Tatva is envisioned in muddy colour; leaves a sweet-sour taste in the mouth.

It is mainly identifiable through the ear since it has a distinct sound.

It is located at Vishuddh Chakra (in the throat region) and it must be experienced in Padmasana while reciting Beejmantra 'Haam'.

Vayu (Air) Tatva

This Tatva activates glands involved in bloating and shrinking of the body. It can be easily identified as at the time of its flow, the airflow in the nostrils moves in a diagonal direction. The maximum length of the exhaled air is 8 fingers and its temperature varies.

This Tatva stays for 8 minutes. This stage is ideal for causing harm to others and dealing with foes through Tantrik mantras even though such negativity is prohibited in all the scriptures. Vayu Tatva makes the mind restless. It can be felt through touch. It tastes sour and the colour is blue. Its seat is Anahat Chakra located in the middle of the chest and close to the heart. Its Sadhna should be done in Padmasana with Beejmantra 'Yaam'.

Agni (Fire) Tatva

Agni is linked to hunger, thirst, sleep, physical growth and laziness. As fire always flows up, in the phase of Agni Tatva the air touches the upper part of the nostrils before being exhaled.

It flows for 12 minutes; its length is 4 fingers; it is warm.

Its accumulation in the breath makes one feel too hungry and causes obesity. It causes anger and greed.

It is mainly seen with eyes – as red colour – and tastes bitter.

Inside the body, it resides in Manipoorak Chakra (close to the navel). Its Sadhna is done in Padmasana and Beejmantra 'Raam'.

Jal (Water) Tatva

This Tatva is responsible for the production of semen, blood, mucus, saliva and urine. Since water always flows down, in this phase, the breath flows down towards the lips. Again when this Tatva is active, the breath measures 16 fingers.

The temperature is low during its existence in the breath for 16 minutes. This Tatva is the most favourable for accomplishing all tasks. During its flow, we can feel the air going deep up to the navel. This Tatva is identifiable through the tongue as a taste.

Under Dhyana it tastes salty; its colour is white or light blue. It is located at Swadhishthan Chakra (five fingers below the navel and three fingers above the groin).

Its asana is Vajrasan and Beejmantra 'Vaam'.

Prithvi (Earth) Tatva

The Prithvi Tatva is responsible for the management of muscle, bone, tendon, cartilage, skin and cells in the body. In this mode, the air flows out from the middle of the nostril and its length is 12 fingers.

This Tatva flows for 20 minutes and the temperature of the air is normal. We can achieve success in anything we do during its flow. Its predominant quality is the smell and, therefore, the organ involved is the nose.

During Dhyana, it is envisioned as yellow in colour and tastes sweet.

Its place in the body is Mooladhar Chakra (two fingers away from the rectum towards the scrotum). Its asana is Vajrasan and Beejmantra is Laam.

The ratio of Tatva in our body is 5 parts earth, 4 parts water, 3 parts fire, 2 parts air and 1 part space.

The Chakras

These days, people in the West are interested in learning about the ancient science of the Seven Chakras of the human body. Many centres have come up where the operators claim to have the capability to invoke the Chakras. What are these Chakras? Simply put, the junction of two or more Nadi is called Chakra. A human body has more than 100 Chakras, including the seven, involving key Nadi like Ida, Pingla and Sushumna.

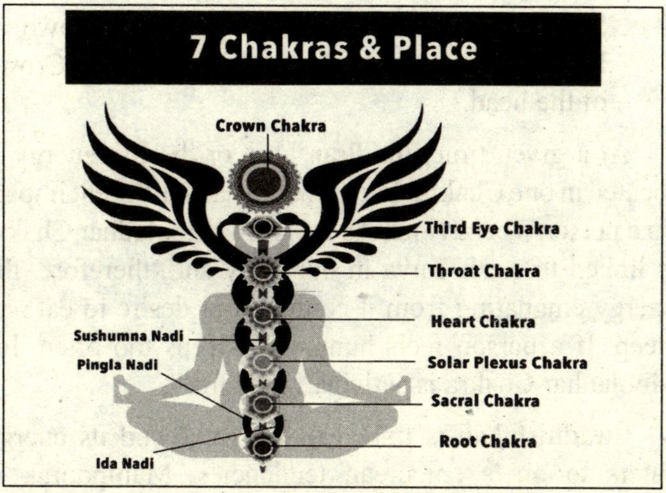

These are:

1. Mooladhar (Root Chakra) – It is located between the rectum and genitals, almost at the base of the spine.

2. Swadhishthan (Sacral Chakra) – Located just two fingers above the genital region.

3. Manipoorak (Solar Plexus Chakra) – Located right below the navel.

4. Anahat (Heart Chakra) – Located in the middle of the chest, right at the joint of the rib cage.

5. Vishudh (Throat Chakra) – Located in the depression of the throat region.

6. Agya (Third eye Chakra) – Located in the middle of the eyebrows.

7. Sahasrara (Crown Chakra) – It's also known as Bramharanadra and is located exactly at the Crown of the head.

At a given time, the Pran Urja or the life energy is located in one Chakra. Each Chakra has a different impact on a person's behaviour. As we know, Mooladhar Chakra is linked to earth Tatva in our body and, therefore, the energy emanating from it controls our desire to eat and sleep. If a person feels hungry or sleeps too often, his Mooladhar Chakra is active all the time.

Swadhishthan is linked to Jal Tatva and its energy caters to one's epicurean tendencies. Manipoorak is linked to Agni Tatva and its energy makes one angry. A person with an overactive Manipoorak Chakra is keen to jump into any situation and get into trouble. Anahata Chakra is linked to Vayu Tatva and its energy makes one generous, peaceful and discreet. Vishudha Chakra is linked to Aakash Tatva and its energy makes one eloquent.

A man's spiritual journey begins at Vishudh Chakra as energy from it starts to get activated towards Agya Chakra. If one is able to steer the energy to Agya Chakra, he attains the peak of his intellectual prowess. From then onwards he takes control of his spiritual journey and can easily straddle through the secrets of spirituality. He remains untouched by material or other possessions and his perspective of life changes.

After Agya Chakra, the energy rises to the final point – The Crown Chakra (Sahasrara Chakra). A person who has steered his energy to Crown Chakra can be likened to a river that becomes sea after merging in it. Such a person has submerged his identity and ego with the Godliness.

There have been a few achievers of this level.

Ramakrishna Paramhansa, Buddha, Nanak, Kabir, Guru Gorakhnath are a few examples. Such humans always spread their aura around.

Prana Vayu (Vital Force of Life)

Prana Vayu, Prana and breathing are synonyms. The inhaled air goes across the body through a network of 10 key Nadis. After entering the body, it gets converted into ten forms of Prana, five of these are key Pranas and the other five are ancillary Pranas.

The five key Pranas are:

1. Prana Vayu: It is located in the heart and manages this key organ of the body.
2. Apan Vayu: It regulates the organs involved in excretion like kidneys, lungs, skin, liver and intestines.
3. Saman Vayu: It is active in the navel region.
4. Udan Vayu: It is active in the throat region.
5. Vyan Vayu: It resides in all the cells of the body.

Ancillary air passages (Sahayak Prana Vayu) are:

1. Naag, responsible for belching.
2. Kurma for movement of eyelids.

3. Krikal, for sneezing.
4. Devdutt, for yawning.
5. Dhananjay, pervades all over the body and remains active for some time even after death. In fact, Devadutt is a very sensitive Prana; it is for this reason that yawning is infectious.

These 10 Prana Vayus move around the body through the Nadi system making their contribution in managing the body functions. Any change in Tatva impacts Prana Vayu. For this reason, Tatvas should always be in balance.

The positive Prana flowing in Pranamarg is responsible for our aura. Have you noticed that we react differently to different people? We instantly like some and dislike others. We instinctively want to speak with someone, even a stranger, and yet have no feeling for others when we meet them. This varied reaction is due to the compatibility or lack of it between the auras of two people. The study of Tatva will make your aura powerful and attract attention.

A person should begin with synchronising his Nadi with sunrise and practice all the exercises for five months. Thereby his Tatva will get balanced and result in the proper management of our Prana Vayu.

RECAP

- Ida and Pingla run for one hour each alternately. For the first 4 minutes of their switching over, Aakash Tatva is actively followed by Vayu, 8 minutes;

Agni, 12 minutes; Jal, 16 minutes and Prithvi for 20 minutes. After an hour the other Nadi gets active with the Aakash Tatva. The cycle continues.

- Ancient texts say that the science of Tatva is the highest form of knowledge. One becomes omniscient after acquiring it.

- Human body has five organs of sense: eye, tongue, nose, skin and ear. Our mind perceives everything through these senses. Likewise, Tatvas can also be identified through these senses: these have colour (to be seen with eyes), taste (felt by mouth), aroma/ flavour (perceived by the nose), texture (by the skin), sound (through the ears).

- The chapter deals with methods of identifying Tatvas through shape, taste, fragrance, feel and sound.

❑❑❑

6

CHAPTER

Astrology and Science of Nadi

The astrology is quite different from the science of Swara. Astrology ascertains the influence of celestial bodies on our life through mathematical calculations. If the place, the date and the time of the birth of an individual furnished to an astrologer are accurate to the second, he would be able to connect these to the position of celestial bodies and accordingly make a horoscope.

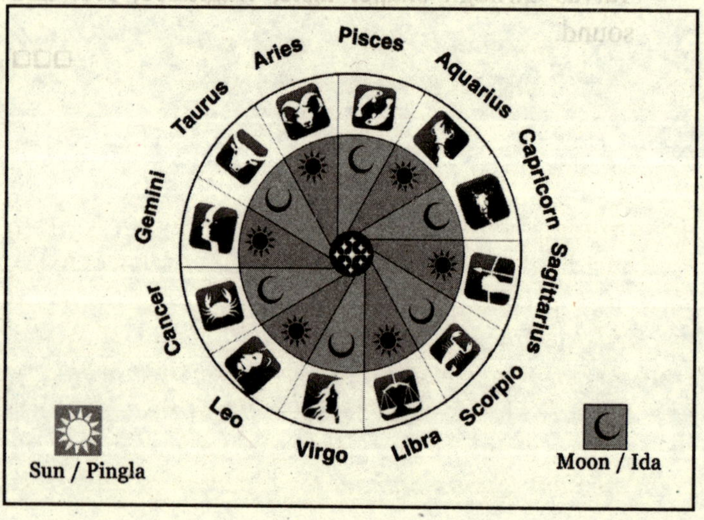

As against the prefixed destiny locked in a horoscope, the science of Swara, helps us coordinate our breath with the movement of celestial bodies by making small changes in our lifestyle.

We have already learnt about the intrinsic link between one's Nadi system and sun and moon; also how it gets disoriented because of lifestyle. Since Nadi is a variable, therefore, not all astrological calculations are effective. In such cases, most astrologers would blame themselves for making wrong calculations.

Lord Shiva explains the link between astrology and the Nadi system as below:

Shloka (Shiva to Parvati)

स्वरहीनः दैवज्ञो नाथहीनं यथा गृहम्।
शास्त्रहीनं यथा वक्त्रं शिरोहीनं च यद्वपुः ॥
साकारे वा निराकारे शुभवायुबलात्कृतम्।
कथयन्ति शुभं केचित्स्वरज्ञाने वरानने ॥

English Translation

An astrologer without the knowledge of Swara is like a house without an owner; speech without knowledge of shastra or a headless body. The science of astrology is incomplete without incorporating the science of Swara. Only an astrologer well versed in Swara Gyan would be able to study the obvious things–in the horoscope – and the not so obvious factors– Nadi–for understanding the right moment (Subha Samay) for a person to undertake a task.

Here is an example: let's assume that as per a person's horoscope his moon is in a strong position. As per this document, his life should be good. However, all predictions based on this will not be valid if that person's Ida has been erratic due to his unnatural routine, bad sleep cycle and unhealthy food habit. What happens if he gets into an altercation at this stage? It might him to commit violence and land him in a police station. If his Ida (linked to Moon) was active at that time, the situation would have been different.

In his case, the Moon will not be favourable to him because of the change in his Nadi. The astrologer's training is to go by the horoscope; he would never realise that the breathing patterns of his client have changed the position of the Moon.

Interestingly, astrology also places sun and moon over all other celestial bodies in impacting our life. For this reason, the Moon is considered an executor of the mind.

Here is another example: a person's horoscope shows the Moon in a powerful position and, therefore, he should be living a good life. However, his Ida has been either non-functional or slow for quite some time and Pingla works overtime. Just think of a situation if he gets into an altercation. Suppose the Agni Tatva is flowing in his Pingla at that time; it would aggravate his anger making him resort to violence and possibly he may.

What went wrong? What made him resort to violence? Was it because of his horoscope or non-functioning Ida?

After all, it was his mind that instructed him to go for violence. If his Ida Nadi (linked to Moon) was active, the situation would have certainly been different.

If the astrologer has no knowledge of Swara, he will take into consideration the changes in Moon's disposition. His advice, therefore, will no longer be valid and least helpful. Astrology holds the Moon as a peg of all calculations. The Moon governs the mind. How will an astrologer's calculation hold the ground if Moon, Ida (in the body) has gone off the track? His calculations would be made from the point of view of Moon's position in his horoscope.

In most cases, astrological calculations go wrong because the client's Nadi has taken an unnatural course. Lord Shiva has told Parvati clearly that an astrologer must also check his client's Nadi. That will help him make accurate predictions and better analysis.

I have no idea how many astrologers today have even the basic idea about Swara. I am sharing my experience with a friend Raj Kumar Sharma, who had made my horoscope 17 years ago. Mr Sharma, a former General Manager with Ashoka Hotel in Delhi, belongs to a family of well-established astrologers. Being a friend, I would often make fun of his predictions. When I was studying and researching for the book, I spoke to him about Swara Gyan. He was surprised and told me he had never heard of it. Being a friend, I advised him to do some exercises to understand the Swara. This would enable him to possibly use his experience for his astrology-related work.

The next day, I received a message from him on my phone: "I practised it… It was miraculous...I shall continue this practice from tomorrow…I will take your advice regarding the effects". Since that day, he has been practising Swara Gyan. He never fails to express his shock at his total ignorance of this science for so long.

The science of Swara is based on logic and facts; its practitioners have real experiences to narrate. For Raj Kumar Sharma, this experience has added a great value to his traditional knowledge.

Shiva continues to elaborate on this to Parvati through this shloka:

Shloka (Shiva to Parvati)

सूर्येण बध्यते सूर्यः चन्द्रश्चन्द्रेण बध्यते।
यो जानाति क्रियामेतां त्रैलोक्यं वशगं क्षणात्॥

English Translation

A human being can control Prana Urja (vital energy) in his body through Pingla Nadi. Likewise, he can control the moon through Ida Nadi. Since the Moon is the executor of the mind; therefore, the mind can be regulated through Ida. One who gains deep knowledge of this through experience can have powers to control the three Lokas – the past, the present and the future.

The energy of the body is regulated by Pingla while Ida regulates the Mind. A person who can regulate his mind and body is, therefore, controls the world. Let's realise that all our sufferings are either due to our body or mind. So, when a person gains controls over both, he can control the past, present and future. In case, the Moon is not in a particularly strong position in one's horoscope, he can work on his Ida and reverse this condition. Lack of knowledge about Nadi would make him suffer.

Take the case of a person who is born with Moon in a strong position. However, later, he adopts an unhealthy lifestyle and spoils his life's equation with the Moon. His mind would generate bad ideas with unpleasant results.

For these reasons, everyone would like to have control over the mind.

In the above shloka, Shiva says that one who understands Ida and Pingla and works on them through Dhyana becomes omniscient and knows all about his past, present and future. I take you back to Devraha Baba who lived up to 250 years. He had told my friend that the secret of his longevity was in 'running Moon in day and Sun in the night'. This made no sense to my friend back then. The following shloka explains what Baba had told him:

Shloka (Shiva to Parvati)

शशाङ्कं वारयेद्रात्रौ दिवा वारयेत्भास्करम्।
इत्याभ्यासरतो नित्यं स योगी नात्र संशयः॥

English Translation

One who is able to stop Ida in the night and Pingla in the day is a yogi.

Here, it is not about regulating but stopping one particular Nadi for 12 hours at a stretch. What Devraha Baba did is no easy task; such a capability of regulating Nadi can be acquired after years of Tapasya.

No householder can do it. However, a family man can use this principle to improve the quality of his life. The science of Swara offers tips for people who cannot afford to do a prolonged Sadhna:

Shloka (Shiva to Parvati)

गुरुशुक्रबुधेन्दूनां वासरे वामनाडिका।
सिद्धिदा सर्वकार्येषु शुक्लपक्षे विशेषत: ॥
अर्काङ्गारकसौरीणां वासरे दक्षनाडिका।
स्मर्तव्या चरकार्येषु कृष्णपक्षे विशेषत: ॥

English Translation

On Mondays, Wednesdays, Thursdays and Fridays of the waxing moon fortnight, one can achieve full success in any task performed during Ida's active phase. This is particularly true for tasks that give a permanent result.

During the waning moon fortnight, all tasks done during the activate phase of Pingla on Sundays, Tuesdays and Saturdays will be successful. The best results will be achieved in tasks of a temporary nature. This could be juxtaposed to the specific period enumerated in a person's horoscope for doing different tasks for the best results.

Shloka (Shiva to Parvati)

अहोरात्रस्य मध्ये तु ज्ञेया द्वादश संक्रमाः ।
वृष-कर्कट-कन्यालि-मृग-मीना निशाकरे ॥
मेषसिंहौ च कुंभश्च तुला च मिथुनं धनुम् ।
उदये दक्षिणे ज्ञेयः शुभाशुभविनिर्णयः ॥

English Translation

Of the 12 sun signs, Taurus, Cancer, Capricorn, Virgo and Pisces are regulated by Ida Nadi (Moon). Others like Aries, Leo, Libra, Gemini, Aquarius and Sagittarius are governed by Pingla (Sun). Various celestial bodies reside in the Nadi during the flow of different Tatva. Like during the flow of Agni Tatva in Pingla, resides Mars; Sun during Prithvi Tatva, Saturn during Jal Tatva, and Rahu during Vayu Tatva. In Ida, Moon resides during the flow of Jal Tatva, Mercury during Prithvi, Jupiter during Vayu and Venus during Agni Tatva. All these combinations are considered ominous.

(Interestingly, for some unexplained reasons, Ketu does not figure in this list.)

One can find the right time for doing a task called Muhurat by simply checking one's sun sign day and Nadi. There is no use doing cumbersome calculations to find the Muhurat.

Here is a glimpse from history about this phenomenon: When raiders looted the wealth of Somnath temple in Dwarka (today's Gujarat), the King wanted to send his army to catch them. However, his purohit advised him against it because his astrological calculations didn't permit this task. As per his calculations, that was not the right moment to go after the enemy.

By the time the auspicious hour came, the bandits were beyond the reach. Swara Gyan does not take into cognizance impractical things like Lagan and Muhurat for initiating a task. Shiva has spoken of the irrelevance of auspicious hour for urgent matters in this shloka:

Shloka (Shiva to Parvati)

न तिथिर्न च नक्षत्रं न वारो ग्रहदेवता: ।
न च विष्टियतीपातो वैधत्याद्यास्तथैव च ॥

English Translation

A Swara Gyani does not need to consider astrological aspects like Muhurat, auspicious date etc. for undertaking a task. He goes by the right combination of Swara and Tatva.

Therefore, it is possible to change the adverse circumstances in life by changing the Nadi. Swara Shastra has directions for astrologers as well. We can, therefore, avoid wasting time in calculating different factors to arrive at the right time to do a task.

Swara Shastra has a lot of tips to offer to astrologers as well. All those pertain to their skill of making predictions. It also has tips to follow in case of a war.

Since these areas are beyond the scope of this work, I am skipping these.

RECAP

- At the time of birth, our Nadis are in perfect coordination with the sun and moon; due to changes in our lifestyle, the Nadis also change course and the system gets disoriented.
- Like sun and moon, other celestial bodies too have an impact on Nadis. Lord Shiva has said an astrologers' knowledge is incomplete without the science of Swara. You can change the course of your life by changing your Nadi for a few days at a stretch.
- In the waxing moon fortnight, during the active stage of Ida, all jobs undertaken on Monday, Wednesday, Thursday and Friday will meet success. It is particularly true for tasks that give permanent results.
- In the fortnight of the waning moon during the flow of Pingla, all jobs undertaken on Sunday, Tuesday and Saturday will be successful. This is particularly true about jobs that yield temporary results. Of the 12 sun signs, Taurus, Cancer, Virgo, Scorpion, Capricorn, and Pisces are regulated by Ida (moon). Aries, Gemini, Leo, Libra, Sagittarius, and Aquarius are regulated by Pingla.
- One can choose a good time to accomplish a task by looking at the combination of one's sun sign, day and the Nadi flow without bothering to ask astrologers for an auspicious moment.

❑❑❑

7

CHAPTER

The Way to Success

The body needs energy the same way a gadget needs electricity to function. Like the electric current, the body energy network also suffers short-circuiting. At night when we sleep, like a battery, our body gets recharged. No matter how much nutritious food one eats, a person cannot live on food alone. In case we do not sleep for two days in a row, the body will give up as sleep is necessary for energizing the body. There is a link between life energy and sleep.

After waking up in the morning, if we set the foot opposite to the active Nadi on the ground, a sharp sensation will pass in the energy circuit of our body. It stays for a nanosecond and, therefore, does not register in our mind. However, its recurrence is harmful. The science of Swara tells us how to avoid this shock.

After waking up, we must check our Nadi before setting out foot on the ground. This means one must set the right foot in case of Pingla and the left in case of Ida. Also, keep in mind that Ida is even and Pingla is odd in nature. So, before leaving the bed, one should slowly touch the ground with the left foot (Ida) even number of times (2-4-6 etc.) and in case of the right foot (Pingla) odd times (1-3-5 etc.). This is because the flow of energy in our body is more on the side of the active Nadi. With this morning drill, one will feel energetic throughout the day.

Likewise, during the passing of urine, you must always activate Ida. This protects us from kidney ailments. While stepping out for the day, take the first step with the foot on the side of active Nadi.

What happens to the body when the Nadi system goes off the track? The following shloka explains it:

Shloka (Shiva to Parvati)

कालत्रये दिनान्यष्टौ विपरीतं यदा बहेत्।
तदा दुष्टफलं प्रोक्तं किंचिन्यूनं तु शोभनम॥
प्रातर्मध्याह्नयोश्चन्द: सायंकाले दिवाकर:।
तदा नित्यं जयो लाभो विपरीतं विवर्जयेत्॥

English Translation

If a person's Nadi does not function in coordination with the Sun and the Moon in the morning, afternoon and evening for eight consecutive days, he is bound to fail in all tasks. Such a person will never become famous. Again if your Ida is functioning at sunrise and midday, and Pingla at sunset, the system is working fine and your success is guaranteed. If not, you are bound to face failures and be a disappointment. If Pingla is malfunctioning, it's better to avoid doing important work on that day.

Nadi System and Chores

One should undertake all assignment that results in irreversible changes when Ida is active. For the best results, it is better to do the work when Jal or Prithvi Tatva is flowing in Ida. The presence of other Tatva will be of no help. This rule is valid only for initiating a task; later on, the Tatva does not matter.

The task to be initiated when Ida is active include long journeys, construction work, fixing a wedding or matchmaking, shopping, consuming nutritious food or medicine, meeting one's boss, making friends, house warming, agriculture work, adopting a Guru, the practice of acting, music, dance or performing arts, helping others and performing yoga.

To make it easier for the readers to remember, let's divide the tasks into two groups: one that requires hard physical labour and the other creative energy of the mind.

The first set of tasks to be performed during Pingla's active phase include swimming, eating, bathing, horse riding, having sex, defeating a foe, the practice of yoga and Sadhna, mountaineering, hypnotism, inspiring others, accepting or giving alms etc. The second set of tasks gives good result when initiated during the flow of Jal or Prithvi Tatva in Ida. These tasks can be done anytime in day or night.

The tasks done during the flow of Prithvi Tatva in both Ida and Pingla give lasting results. Jal Tatva too gives a guaranteed success. Jobs done during the flow of Vayu Tatva meet partial success. However, undertaking a job in the Agni or Aakash Tatva will surely result in a major failure. Aakash Tatva is best-suited for Dhyana and prayers.

The above tips might confuse you. Just remember the first time you wanted to ride a bicycle. You would sit on it, touch its handle and peddle yet could not ride it till one day, it moved and then cycling came naturally to you.

Thereafter, you never had to apply your mind to ride it. So, the first step to ride the bicycle was to make an effort. No amount of preaching could make that happen; it was your practice of balancing that made you do this.

Similarly, with regular practice, one would soon begin to understand the Nadi and Tatva. In fact, it is easier than cycling since breathing is a round-the-clock activity while cycling is not. Besides, unlike cycling its practice does not result in fall and injuries.

Since the flow of energy in our body and mind is greater on the side of the active Nadi, we must do important tasks like money transaction, meeting the boss or a friend with the hand on the side of active Nadi. It creates a positive perception about you in the mind of the person in front of you.

In case you feel that your interaction is not going well and it is a waste of time, you should change your position to ensure the other person is on the side of your inactive Nadi as you speak with him. Soon you will find he wants to end the meeting, maybe by claiming something important had come up and sought your leave. You just have to slightly change your position and take a sitting pose.

Women are better in use of Ida because of its feminine nature while men can do the same with Pingla, the masculine Nadi. This is because a woman's brain is more active on the left side, while a man's is on the right. Both of them have the same form of life energy in a dominant position and these are opposite in men and women. For this reason, the two sexes complement each other; their combined life energies create complete energy. This is also the reason for attraction between opposite sexes. So, if a man is face-to-face with his lady boss or a friend, he would make a good impression if he uses his Pingla and a woman facing a man by using Ida.

Please note that the Ida and Pingla are on the opposite sides starting from the Mooladhar Chakra but ultimately meet together at the Agya Chakra, (Refer to the image given) hence it does not apply in case of nostrils. For both men and women, the left nostril is Ida and the right nostril is Pingla.

The science of Swara lists tips as important as how to escape bandits and thieves and punishment from a king etc. These acts are irrelevant in the modern-day, yet one can use these for a different set of actions. For example, if we sense danger Opposite System of Nadi for men & women coming from a person sitting on the side of our active Nadi, we can shift position to keep him on the side of our inactive Nadi.

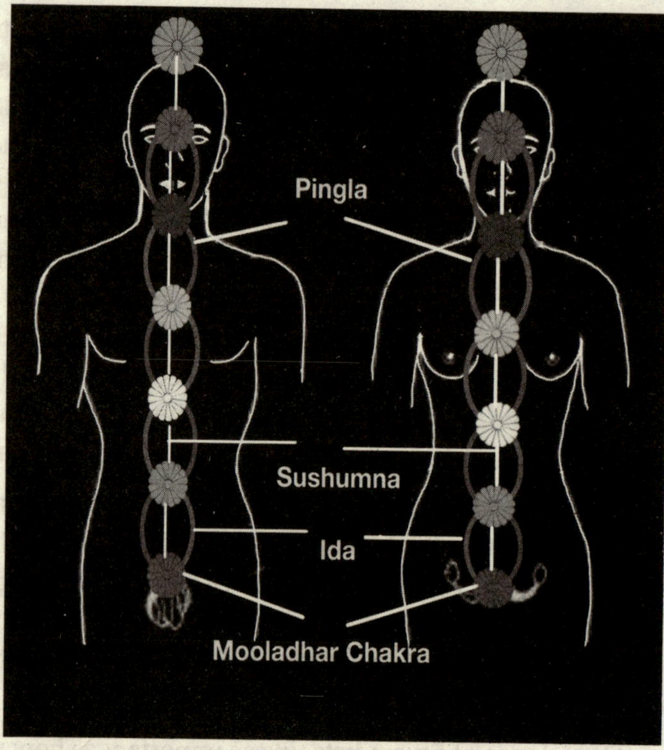

This can be tried with persons whom we do not like and yet have to face them daily. By positioning such a person on the side of your inactive Nadi; you will find the person has found someone else to interact with. On the contrary, when you are facing someone who does not like you, it is good to keep him on the side of your active Nadi. It will work magic and you will soon be friends with him.

While praying in a religious place, we must make a wish to the Almighty while inhaling. If we do the same while exhaling, it is never answered. Remember, you just have to initiate your prayer while inhaling. However, prayer can be said anytime, irrespective of Nadi or Tatva.

Sushumna Nadi and Tasks

Sushumna is active for a brief period – approximately four-five minutes – during the Ida-Pingla changeover. It is difficult to identify it. The breath in Sushumna coming from both the nostrils is about four-finger long.

All Tatva flow one after the other in the breath during Sushumna's phase. If you initiate a task when Agni or Aakash Tatva is flowing, you are bound to fail. Therefore, it is better not to undertake any task during this phase.

Sushumna is also called Shunya (Zero) Swara, due to its propensity for destruction. Ancient texts describe Sushumna as a poison that can destroy all the result of our hard work. During its phase, the results will be always contrary to one's wishes. One should never start a journey at the beginning of Sushumna's active phase as it is bound to end in a mishap. However, it is most suited for Dhyana, prayers or any spiritual practice.

Sushumna is the meeting point of Ida and Pingla or sun and moon. It begins soon after the last split second of Ida. Soon Sushumna lapses into its end activating Pingla. In spiritual terms, the meeting point of Ida and Sushumna and not the meeting of the day and night is called Sandhya. Here is a Shloka about it:

Shloka (Shiva to Parvati)

न संध्या संधिरित्याहु: संध्या संधिर्निगद्यते।
विषम: संधिग: प्राण स संधिज: संधिरुच्यते॥

English Translation

The meeting of day and night is not Sandhya; it's just the optics. In real terms, the flow of Swara in Sushumna is called Sandhya. This is formed by the meeting of two Swara. Therefore, one should only pray or meditate during this period.

Shloka (Parvati to Shiva)

देव देव महादेव सर्वसंसारतारक।
स्थितं त्वदीयहृदये रहस्यं वद मे प्रभो॥

English Translation

Lord, please tell me more about this science.

Shloka (Shiva to Parvati)

स्वरज्ञानरहस्यात्तु न काचिच्चेष्टदेवता।
स्वरज्ञानरतो योगी स योगी परमो मत:॥

English Translation

O beautiful one, the science of Swara is the top-secret and the highest level of knowledge; a yogi who is busy in its practice is the greatest one.

RECAP

- In the morning before moving out of the bed, one must place the foot on the ground on the side of the active Nadi.
- If at sunrise and noon, your Ida is active, and at sunset, Pingla, you will rock during the day. If the Nadi system remains disoriented for eight days in a row, one would fail in everything. Fame will never touch him.
- Ida Nadi is most suitable for starting a long journey, construction work, fixing a marriage, wedding, shopping, meeting your friend or boss, house warming, acquiring a Guru, practising science, helping others, practising performing arts like dance, acting, singing, music or art yoga.
- Pingla remains most suitable for initiating physical exercise like swimming, eating, bathing, having sex, defeating an enemy, motivating others, giving or accepting alms, practising hypnotism, tantra vidhya, motivating others, etc.
- The Agni Tatva in Sushumna is akin to death. This phase is best for meditation.

❑❑❑

8

CHAPTER

The Length of Breath

Prana Vayu or the Life Force Energy protects the body the way soldiers guard a fort. Like a loyal and trusted friend, it remains with us right from birth till our end as a shield against diseases and ailments. However, due to our object lack of awareness, we do not value it and often make mistakes. We tend to behave like a trader who continues to suffer losses each day by spending more than his earning and eventually goes bankrupt.

Normally, the inhaled breath is ten-finger long.

However, when we exhale, the Prana Vayu is 12-finger long. This means, like the trader, we are exhaling more than we inhale and the body is making losses. This makes us age faster and also hastens our end. Just remember, it is not about the amount of air inhaled or exhaled; only the length of the breath.

The length varies as per the workout:

During brisk walking the exhaled air measures: 22-24 fingers, Running: 36-42 fingers, Getting angry: 45-50 fingers, Sex-making: 55-60 fingers. Sleeping: 60-70 fingers, while eating or vomiting: 16-17 fingers.

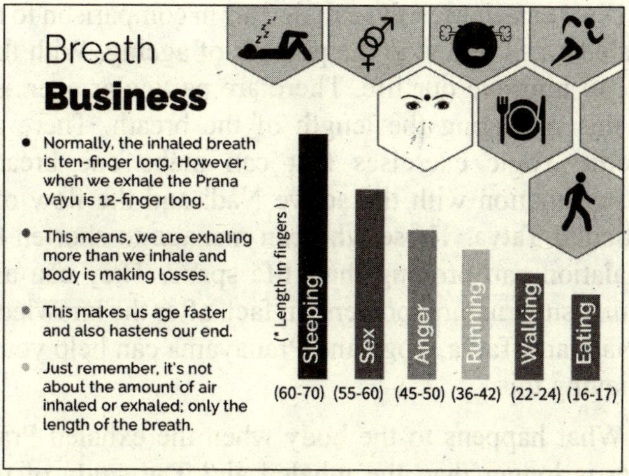

The inhaled air rarely exceeds 10 fingers while the air being exhaled varies to a point that at times, it can hit the person facing you. For this precise reason, most ancient texts prescribe control over the desire for sex and anger. These actions involving heavy breathing out weaken one's vital force for life (Prana Urja Shakti).

A Chinese man who lived up to 165 years revealed the secrets of his longevity as breathing in deep up to the navel and exhaling fully and always keeping his spine straight. Both these are important elements of Pranayama (a set of exercise to regulate our breathing) and yet we never pay attention to deep breathing. The Thumb rule for good breathing is that while inhaling abdomen should rise like a balloon and not shrink in. About 90 per cent of humans do breathing the wrong way: their abdomen shrinks while inhaling and bloats while exhaling. There are specific exercises to practice this in Pranayama called Kumbhak, Purak and Rechak.

If we can shorten the exhaled air in comparison to the inhaled air, it will stop the process of ageing. With this, we can improve our life. There are particular exercises for this managing the length of the breath. There are specific Yogic exercises that can make one breathe in coordination with the active Nadi and the flow of a particular Tatva. Those who can manage to shorten the exhalation can prolong their life spans. They can also acquire supernatural powers. In fact, after the knowledge of Nadi and Tatva, Yoga and Pranayama can help you in achieving this.

What happens to the body when the exhaled Prana Vayu is longer than the inhaled air? The study of this is interesting. As per the science of Swara, if a person is able to reduce the length of exhaled vital air by one finger, he loses all his desires (the cause of misery); if by two fingers, he reaches the pinnacle of bliss or happiness, three fingers make him powerful poet/writer, four fingers make him a great orator, five fingers gives him the power of clairvoyance, and six to seven fingers make him as powerful as a wind. If he can reduce his breath by eight fingers he would achieve the ultimate –the eight Siddhis.

Siddhi, in Sanskrit, means perfection or accomplishment. As per spiritualism, the eight Siddhis are described below.

What are 8 Siddhis ?

Many ancient Indian scriptures, including Swara Shastra, speak of eight Siddhis. 'Hanuman Chalisa' also refers to the Lord as the "Ashta siddhi nav nidhi ke daata" (the giver of new treasure in the form of eight Siddhis). What is a Siddhi? What is their use? Do these make a practitioner omnipresent; and give him powers to become the smallest and the largest form at will.

It sounds incredible that a person can become invisible, turn into a tiny entity, or as large as he wants to be at will provided he is a practitioner of Siddhi. The shastra or ancient texts have conveyed many valuable bits of knowledge in hidden form, (Refer to chapter-2-3). This form of writing with concealed meaning is called Kshepak and it is used deliberately. It's impossible to know the meaning of many texts by reading and translating. Therefore one needs a Guru, the guide, who is a practitioner and has experienced the knowledge through Sadhna to interpret the texts.

Before we know about Siddhi, we must understand a few more things.

We generally consider the human body in the physical form that we see it as. However, the body is in two other forms too – one is the ASTRAL BODY and the other the CAUSAL BODY.

Atma (soul) is beyond and above these three body forms and 5 sheaths called Panch Kosha.

Panch Kosha can be likened to layers of onion, close and yet distinct layers. These are:

1. Annmay Kosha or the food sheath

2. Pranmay Kosha or the vital sheath

3. Manomay Kosha or the mental sheath
4. Vigyanmay Kosha or the intellectual sheath
5. Anandmay Kosha of the sheath of the bliss

Annmay Kosha: Food regulates our physical body while Pranmay Kosha is regulated by the breath. The latter (Pranmay Kosha) is very important since it's active in all 5 Koshas and three bodies. In no time, the breath travels across three bodies, panch kosha, and makes cursory contact with soul (pure consciousness) and returns.

This means that each intake of breath touches the soul. Since the contact happens for a split second, we fail to experience it and it's not registered by the mind that is constantly preoccupied with thoughts.

One can try this experiment: Track your breath to a point where it makes a U-turn for exiting. Though it seems an easy task we fail to record it because our mind interrupts us with its incessant thoughts and ideas. In the ancient scripture 'Vigyan Bhairav Tantra', this is cited as a key impediment in reaching the sutra (formula) to attain the ultimate spiritual goal.

Let's do another exercise: Hold your breath as long as possible. You will notice that your thoughts has also stopped. At the most, the mind is thinking of when do I restart breathing. By holding the breath, the flow of vital energy in Manomay Kosha also stops. For this reason, slowing of breath also makes the mind calmer and slows the flow of thoughts. This makes the mind rest and get fresh. Manomay Kosha is connected to all the seven levels of the mind (Refer to chapter- 11).

The next sheath is Vigyanmay Kosha. It's a repository of unlimited Intellect. However, this is just a fraction of our real intellect that deals in logic and cognitive power and can argue. The consciousness of a normal human being can only barely touch the Vigyanmay kosha.

A fraction of the unlimited intellect located in Vigyanmay kosha is enough to a Newton and an Einstein. However, even realization is rare or we would have had so many Einsteins and Newtons. In his last moments, Einstein is said to have admitted that what he has learned in life is too little because he doesn't even know what all is there to learn. Such thought could only come from a person whose consciousness is connected to Vigyanmay kosha.

To put it simply, awareness, the mindfulness creates consciousness and the growth of consciousness creates intellect. That is why only Newton thought about the reason behind the apple's falling and wondered why it didn't fall left, right, or even skywards. By going into this basic reality, he discovered the Law of Gravity. The apple would fall even before Newton was born. Why others didn't notice it?

Ahankar (Ego) germinates from the vanity of being intellectuals with our (limited) intellect. It's the ego and it makes us feel different from others and especially divinity. For this reason, we always consider the physical body, mind and limited intellect as self-existence.

With such faculties, forget about reaching Vigyanmay Kosha we won't even reach the kosha located below it. Human birth is meant for the growth of consciousness.

Last one, Anandmay Kosha is related to the feeling of bliss or ecstasy. It's connected to our causal body. The feeling of bliss or ecstasy is experienced by the Causal body behind which the soul is located.

We experience bliss only when we go deeper into something and touch the soul close to the Causal body. In simple terms when we go deeper into a thing that gives pleasure, our mind stops thinking or in other words, we give up thinking about ourselves.

For example, watching a scene in a movie, listening to favourite music, or soaking our senses in a fragrance we feel very happy. During sexual activity, we experience extreme pleasure and give up our ego. In this, the consciousness reaches the Causal body.

At this, we get a glimpse of the soul located behind the Causal body. This is ecstasy and in this stage, we lose track of our physical and even Astral body. The more we lose the sense of 'our self' the more pleasure we get.

This makes it clear that pleasure cannot be searched for; it is obtained by losing the sense of self. However, we still don't have the experience of extreme bliss (Parmanand) because we have reached close and not yet to the soul.

Under normal circumstances, we cannot experience the soul that lay behind so many sheaths of panch koshas.

We have to do Sadhna to attempt that. It's in Dhyana that we can forget about our ego.

The Astral body is an entity that gets into the physical body riding on the soul. It's also called Jeevatma. On death, the physical body is destroyed but the Causal body and Astral body are indestructible. The Astral body is reborn and gets a physical body. Only when the Astral body gets destroyed does one get freed from the cycle of life and death, called MOKSHA. Most of the experiments in Sadhna are related to the Astral body.

Why do we feel our existence is only with the physical body? This is because the Astral body is not ready to part with the physical body at any cost. The Astral body has gone through cycles of death and rebirth and therefore understands the importance of the physical body and is afraid of losing it yet again. For this reason, the Astral body govern our mind through Manomay Kosha and makes our mind think that the physical body is 'us'.

The Astral body is unhappy if we try to connect with soul (pure consciousness). Astral body knows a glimpse of the soul would make it redundant. So, the body too makes excuses for doing Sadhna.

Whenever we want to do any such Sadhna, which makes us try to connect with soul (pure consciousness), in the same way our Astral body gets scared. Because Astral body knows a glimpse of the soul would make it redundant. Therefore, in order to save itself, the Astral body starts looking for excuses to avoid spiritual practice through the mind.

A human being has immense latent powers. These are invoked only in extreme emergencies like the existential threat. In normal circumstances, the power is latent and only comes into play when a person is faced with a near-death situation. Under normal circumstances and without a compelling reason, it remains inert.

In the modern jargon, Siddhi is thus the process of activating the downloaded and installed, and yet inactive software inside a human being.

Psychologists also say that most of the time, only two percent of the human mind is active; the rest remains inactive and unused. Think of it: a human mind of which only a fraction of the capacity is in use can create wonders, what happens if all its capacity is utilized and unleashed.

As per biology, a part of the body that remains in disuse for a long time becomes redundant and loses its function. If we don't use our limbs and organs like hands, eyes, ears, etc. for a long time these will become non-functional. Likewise, a human being lives his life span sleeping and without invoking his latent faculties. He dies and is reborn without this realization.

Only a strong desire can invoke the latent power. The question arises: what part of us should desire it? Desire is born in the mind and it's not in our control. It's therefore recommended in all religions that humans should do Sadhna to rein in the mind through regulation of the five senses. The mind is diverted by the Astral body that has an interest in keeping a human away from reaching the soul.

The human body referred to in the Siddhis is not about the human form we see; it's about the invisible and two more entities: one the Causal body and the other the Astral body. The latter controls the mind. Unless this concept is understood one may not be able to follow many other aspects.

A practitioner can overpower his causal and astral bodies and even travel across seas. Telepathy uses this maneuver. Let's analyze the eight Siddhis: (as written in Shastra)

1. **Anima:** This makes one see his body as a particle or an atom. The practitioner of this Siddhi can convert his body into an atom at will.

2. **Mahima:** The practitioner of this Siddhi can expand his body as big as the universe.

3. **Garima:** This Siddhi gives powers to its practitioner to increase the weight of his body to a level that nobody and no power on earth can move it.

4. **Laghima:** The practitioner can make his body as light as air and can move faster than the wind. He can enter any other body under its nano size.

5. **Prapti:** The practitioner has the power to become invisible.

6. **Prakayam:** The practitioner of this Siddhi can read the mind of a person.

7. **Ishita:** This Siddhi makes one Godly. Its practitioner thus becomes God-like and omnipresent. He can have control of everything happening in the Universe.

8. **Vashita:** The practitioner of this Siddhi can control the mind of another person, living and non-living beings. Such an achiever can influence any person and the events on the earth.

Just to remind the reader that all these Siddhis can be practiced by decreasing the length of the breath. In Swara Shastra says that by reducing the length of one's breath to less than eight-finger, one can achieve eight Siddhis. However, this needs further elucidation.

If a Yogi is able to reduce his exhaled breath by 12 fingers, he remains alive even without breathing in a meditative state and reaches the pinnacle of Samadhi (ultimate stage of Dhyana).

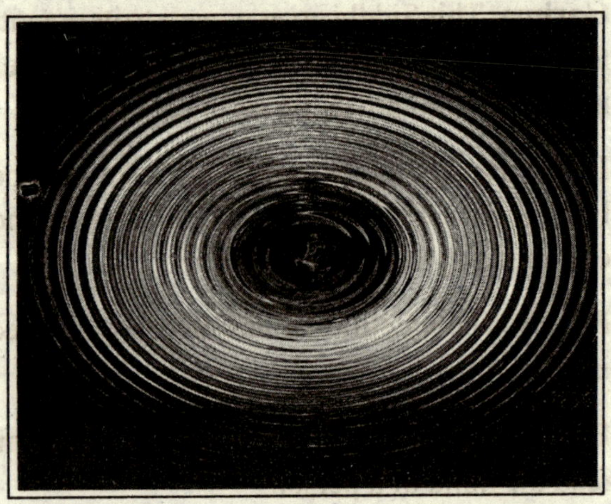

While understanding this, one has to make a clear distinction between genuine practitioners and charlatans. The latter would dig a big hole in the earth and get inside in full public view only to emerge alive after four days. The public would believe in this Baba's extraordinary powers. The fact is such people are conmen; they keep breathing through a network of pipes. Their only purpose to stage this show is to impress others. The genuine people never make an exhibition of their stage of Sadhna. Such Yogis have no urge to impress others; they do it for nurturing their souls and self-realisation. Have a look at the following Shloka:

Shloka (Shiva to Parvati)

द्वादशे हंसचारश्च गङ्गामृतरसं पिबेत्।
आनखाग्रं प्राणपूर्णे कस्य भक्ष्यं च भोजनम्॥
एवं प्राणविधिः प्रोक्तः सर्वकार्यफलप्रदः।
ज्ञायते गुरुवाक्येन न विद्याशास्त्रकोटिभिः॥

English Translation

By reducing the length of the exhaled vital air by 12 fingers, the yogi achieves immortality. In real terms, it means he will remain alive in the stage of dhyana even when he's not breathing. And the Yogi has absolute control over his body; he conquers his bodily needs like food and other desires.

This is the last stage of Sadhna. One can get a lot of information from the ancient texts on regulating the breath. However, it must be kept in mind that information is not knowledge. One can learn to have control over his vital energy only with the guidance of a Guru. I strictly forbid readers from self-learning this; a small mistake can land one in a major problem. This is the reason why I am not explaining the methods of practising this Sadhna.

Dangers of a Disoriented Nadi

Nadi undergoes changes before the onset of a disease. If we know about it and are aware, we could prevent it. Ailments attack the body when a part of it is weak. The thumb rule is: a change in breathing pattern is a signal of a disease that is about to attack the body. After the disease has hit you, identify the Nadi the active phase of which aggravates the symptoms.

Thereafter, activate the other Nadi for quick relief. In case you are feeling pain, check the Nadi and lay down on the same side in order to activate your other Nadi. This will give you instant relief. Dangers of a disoriented Nadi system are enumerated in the following Shlokas:

Shloka (Shiva to Parvati)

रात्रौ चन्द्रो दिवा सूर्यो बहेद्यस्य निरन्तरम्।
जानीयात्तस्य वैमृत्युः षट्मासाभ्यन्तरे भवेत्॥
अहोरात्रद्वयं यस्य पिङ्गलायां सदा गतिः।
तस्य वर्षद्वयं प्रोक्तं जीवितं तत्त्ववेदिभिः॥
त्रिरात्रं वहते यस्य वायुरेकपुटे स्थितः।
तदा संवत्सरायुस्तं प्रवदन्ति मनीषिणः॥

रात्रौ चन्द्रो दिवा सूर्यो बहेद्यस्य निरन्तरम्।
जानीयात्तस्य वैमृत्युः षट्मासाभ्यन्तरे भवेत्॥
शरीरं शीतलं यस्य प्रकृतिर्विकृता भवेत्।
तदरिष्टं समासेन व्यासतस्तु निबोध मे॥

English Translation

If a person is experiencing his one Nadi continuously functioning for 24 hours (day and night), he would die in three years.

When a person feels his Pingla is functional round-the-clock for many days, he is destined to die in two years.

If someone is experiencing his one Nadi has been continuously functioning for three days, he is destined to die in a year.

If a person is breathing through his left nostril in the night and through the right in the day for many days, he would not live long.

Under all the above circumstances, if his body begins to become cold and his condition deteriorates, it's the sign of an impending tragedy.

Shloka (Shiva to Parvati)

हुंकारो शीतलो यस्य फुत्कारो वह्निसन्निभः।
महावैद्यो भवेद्यस्य तस्य मृत्युर्भवेद्ध्रुवम्॥
एकादिषोडषा हानिर्यदि भानुर्निरन्तरम्।
वहेद्यस्य भवेन्मृत्युः शेषाहेन मासिकम्॥
सम्पूर्णं वहते सूर्यश्चन्द्रमा नैव दृश्यते।
पक्षेण जायते मृत्युः कालज्ञेनानुभाषितम्॥
मूत्रं पुरीषं वायुश्च समकालं प्रवर्तते।
तदाऽसौ चलितो ज्ञेयो दशाह्ले म्रियते ध्रुवम्॥
सम्पूर्णं वहते चन्द्रः सूर्यो नैव च दृश्यते।
मासेन जायते मृत्युः कालज्ञेनानुभाषितम्॥

English Translation

If a person is inhaling cool air and exhaling very warm air, he can't escape death, at any cost.

If a person's Pingla works continuously for 16 days, he will only survive till the end of the month.

If a person's Pingla is on for 15 days continuously and the left Swara is inert, he would die in a few days.

If a person passes his stools, urine and fart at the same time for many days, it is a signal of his end being near.

If a person's Pingla is flowing continuously and the Ida is inert for days together, he would live only a few months.

> **NOTE:**
> Swara Shastra does not offer an explanation for the above conclusions

Child Bearing and Breathing

Swara Shastra was written in a male-dominant era. Back then, women's role in society was confined to looking after the home and bearing and raising children. For this reason, this text has many Shlokas that were written keeping in mind only the male mindset.

Today, women are equal to men in all spheres. We all stand for gender equality. For this reason, I am not highlighting the misogynistic writings of this Shastra.

I am only focusing on portions that are relevant to the process of childbearing.

A woman can get pregnant between the fourth to the 16th day of her monthly menstrual cycle. According to ancient texts, the forbidden dates for childbearing are the first three days after the fresh cycle and the first, third, eighth and, 15th day of both the lunar fortnights. A child born on these days will face problems. Once again, you should remember that you can activate Ida by lying down on the right side and Pingla by lying down on the left side. Here are shlokas related to childbearing:

Shloka (Shiva to Parvati)

ऋतुस्नाता रता नारी पञ्चमैह्वि यदा भवेत्।
सूर्यचन्द्रमसोर्योगे सेवनात्पुत्र संभवः॥

English Translation

On the fifth day of the fresh menstrual cycle, if the woman's Ida and the man's Pingla are active during conjugation, the child born of this union will be a boy.

Shloka (Shiva to Parvati)

सुषुम्ना सूर्यवाहेन ऋतुदानं तु योजयेत्।
अङ्गीनः पुमान्यस्तु जायतैत्र कुविग्रहः॥
ऋत्वारम्भे रविः पुंसां स्त्रीणां च सुधाकरः।
उभयोः सङ्गमे प्राप्तो वन्ध्या पुत्रमवाप्नुयात्॥
ऋत्वारम्भे रविः पुंसां शुक्रान्ते च सुधाकरः।
अनेन क्रमयोगेन नादत्ते कामिनीजनः॥
शून्ये शून्यं युगे युग्मं गर्भपातश्च संक्रमे।
तत्त्ववित्स विजानीयात् कथितं तत्तु सुन्दरि॥
गर्भाधानं मारुते स्याच्च दुःखी दिक्षु ख्यातो वारुणे सौख्ययुक्तः।
गर्भस्रावः स्वल्पजीवश्च वह्नौ भोगी भव्यः पार्थिवेनार्थयुक्तः॥
धनवान् सौख्ययुक्तश्च भोगवानर्थ संस्थितिः।
स्यान्नित्यं वारुणे तत्त्वेव्योम्नि गर्भो विनश्यति॥

English Translation

If on the fifth day of a woman's menstrual cycle her Sushumna and the man's Pingla are active, the child born out of this union will be without a limb and ugly- looking.

At the beginning of the menstrual cycle, the union between an infertile woman with her Ida and a man with his Pingla active can result in childbearing.

If a Man's Pingla is active and during copulation, suddenly his Ida gets active, the union will not result in pregnancy. If a man and a woman mate during the active phase of their Sushumna, the child is not conceived.

However, if the Tatvas flowing in their respective Sushumnas coincide, the pregnancy will result in the conception of twins. Also, if the Nadi of both man and woman change during copulation, the conception may happen but the pregnancy will end in abortion.

A child conceived during the flow of Vayu Tatva will be irreligious and unlucky; in Jal Tatva, happy and proud; in Agni Tatva have a short life. The one born of the union at the time of flow of Prithvi Tatva will have a life of abundance and luxuries.

The child born out of the union at the time of the flow of Jal Tatva will have a life of abundance and luxury while it's impossible for a woman to become pregnant if she mates during the flow of Aakash Tatva.

Shloka (Shiva to Parvati)

महीन्द्रे सुसुतोत्पत्तिर्वारुणे दुहिता भवेत्।
शेषेषु गर्भहानिः स्याज्जातमात्रस्य वा मृतः ॥

English Translation

A male child will be conceived if a woman mates during the flow of Prithvi Tatva and it will be a girl if it's Jal Tatva. In the other three Tatva, the pregnancy does not occur; if it happens the child born will have a short life.

The Kings and emperors, therefore, consulted experts for time and day of which they should try for the conception in order to have a child with the choicest qualities. It is another matter that this privilege was enjoyed only by the powerful Kings and not by the general public.

RECAP

- The length of the inhaled breath is 10 fingers and exhaled air is 12 fingers. Mind you, it is about the length and not the volume of the air going in or out.
- In certain acts, the length of the exhaled air is much longer than of the inhaled air. While doing a brisk walk, the length of the exhaled breath is 22-24 fingers, while running 36-42, getting angry 45-50, having sex 55-60, and while sleeping 60-70 fingers. While eating and vomiting, it becomes 16-17 fingers long.
- In some actions, we barely inhale breath that's ten- finger long. However, breath exhaled is much longer. For this reason, all the ancient texts ask humans to abstain from sex and anger. These actions weaken our Prana Vayu, the vital life force.
- If we can manage to shorten the exhaled Prana Vayu, you can increase your life; you can also become empowered with divine siddhis.
- While inhaling our stomach must bloat and get sucked inside while exhaling. Most of us do this in reverse and the wrong way. Always breathe in till navel.
- The change in Nadis gives us a signal of impending disease or death. Knowledge about this can help avert both.

❑❑❑

9

CHAPTER

Sadhna and Breathing

Sadhna is the regimen of a personalized and experience-based study of anything. Can we do Sadhna of breathing? Interestingly, breathing is part of all our activities including Sadhna. A bowler holds his breath while throwing the ball to the batsman in the cricket ground; a batsman takes a deep breath before facing the ball. A goalkeeper in hockey or football holds his breath for a second as he charges to defend the goal. During swimming, one has to breathe underwater and then lift his head above the surface for deep breathing. In archery or shooting, a player holds his breath while hitting the target. A weight lifter also holds his breath while lifting the weight; he will fail to lift the requisite weight in case he chooses to exhale.

From the above examples, it is clear that we have to regulate breath while doing various actions. It is another matter that most of us are ignorant about the basic fact that all actions revolve around breathing.

In Sadhna too, breathing is the key. Sadhna is not about the rituals of lighting an incense stick or a lamp. The Rishis never cared about such things; instead, they choose the solitude of forests and mountains, closed their eyes to the outer world to begin their inner journey by controlling their breathing.

Although in ancient texts, the secrets of breathing pop up as capsules of allusions and are, therefore, difficultto understand for a casual reader. It is only after rigorous Sadhna that one experiences and understands the deeper and hidden meanings in these texts.

For example, let's take a Sanskrit word 'Hansachar' (Chapter 8, Shloka 1). This word is very important for the study of Indian traditions of spiritualism. In fact, one could end up writing a book explaining this one word. Swara Shastra has a lot of veiled information about this word and its meaning but it is sparingly used. It is used only to explain that a Sadhak (one who does Sadhna) who can reduce his exhaled Prana Vayu by 12 fingers should be considered as having attained immortality. However, even while referring Hansachar, the author neither explains the meaning of the word nor the method of reaching immortality. As has been said above, the writers of this Shastra made a conscious decision to ensure the secrets in it would be known only to the genuine seekers of knowledge.

For this reason, they split all the key information over different shlokas and pages. The idea of staggering the information in a manner that confuses an ordinary reader was deliberate so that only those deeply interested would take pains to read the book and be able to join the dots. The seeker of information has to be stubborn and determined.

How this was done will be clear by analysing the word Hansachar as used in the Shastra. Sanskrit word 'Hansa' comprises two sounds: 'Hun' and 'Sah', and both are verbs. Aachar means 'by doing so'. Hansachar is, therefore, hun+sah+aachar and means the action of doing Huns. What is the action of 'Huns'? The exhalation is accompanied by the sound 'hun' and inhalation by 'Sah'. A Sadhak can clearly hear these sounds in Sadhna. It means that Sadhna begins by uttering these sounds. As he gets deeper into Sadhna, his breathing slows significantly; and at this stage, he experiences the sound of 'Hans'.

In Sadhna if one starts listening to the sound of the air being exhaled till the beginning of inhalation it would be Huns; if we start listening in reverse, we will hear Soham. In spiritualism, both these sounds 'Huns' and 'Soham' are very important words. Lakhs of devotees chant these mantras. I believe most of them have no idea that these are the basic sounds of the breath and not the word that they believe it is. They also do not realise that it happens only through breathing and the process is called Hansachar.

At this stage, Sushumna gets active with Aakash Tatva flowing and the length of the breath is four fingers. Gradually, the practitioner further shortens it.

Since we have decoded the word Hansachar it will be easier for readers to understand many other shlokas. Let's learn the meaning of the following shlokas that are strewn around on different pages in Swara Shastra:

Shloka (Shiva to Parvati)

हकारस्य सकारस्य विना भेदं स्वरः कथम्।
सोहं हंसपदेनैव जीवो जपति सर्वदा॥

English Translation

None can get the knowledge of Swara without learning about the secrets of 'Hakar' and 'Sakar'. Only through a continuous recitation of 'Soham' or 'Hansa', one can get the full knowledge of Swara.

In the lingo of Spiritualism, 'Hakar' stands for 'Hun' and 'Sakar' for 'Sah'.

It is interesting to note that in this Shloka, it is made clear that no Swara Gyan can be acquired without knowing about 'Hun' and 'Sah' while both the terms are not explained. Had I not explained these, the readers would have never understood the meaning of the above shloka. This explanation is given in yet another shloka on a different page in Swara Shastra!

Shloka (Shiva to Parvati)

हकारो निर्गमे प्रोक्त सकारेण प्रवेशणम्।
हकारः शिवरूपेण सकारः शक्तिरुच्यते॥

English Translation

The exhalation is accompanied by the sound 'Hun' while inhalation by 'Sah'. 'Hun' symbolizes Shiva and the 'Sah' Shakti.

With this, readers can understand the mystery of Hans and Soham. In all texts, the recitation of 'Hans' and 'Soham' is considered sacred. Many Gurus give this a secret mantra for chanting to their disciples. This sound does not have to be uttered; in a consciously breathing process, it comes naturally with inhalation and exhalation. During the run of Sushumna, at the point of the union between Ida and Pingla and within this comes a moment when the incoming and outgoing breath is juxtaposed. That precise point is the union of 'Hun' and 'Sah' alias Hans.

Paramhansa is the title prefixed to the names of those who have achieved higher spiritual levels. They are therefore rated as 'above the Hansa'. Ramakrishna Paramahansa, the Guru of Swami Vivekananda, is an example.

Sadhna is linked to the seven Chakras that are located at the cross-section of the Nadi. Specific Beej Mantras (seed chants) mentioned in the chapter on Tatvas are used to invoke these Chakras (details in the Chapter 14).

In the Shlokas below, Shiva is giving tips on Sadhna to Parvati. These shlokas also unravel many secrets. Many of you may know about the importance of taking a bath in the water of the Ganga. You must have also heard about Sangam in Prayag where Kumbha Mela is organized and thousands of people participate in it. Do you know what do Ganga, Yamuna and Saraswati denote in spiritualism? Also, where is Prayag located on the map of the spiritual journey? Here are some shlokas that can explain this:

Shloka (Shiva to Parvati)

रक्षणीयस्ततो देहो यतो धर्मादिसाधनम्।
योगाभ्यासात्समायान्ति साधुयाप्यास्तु साध्यताम्।
असाध्या जीवितं घ्नन्ति न तत्रास्ति प्रतिक्रिया॥

English Translation

Our body is a resource of dharma; we must therefore protect it by practising Yoga every day. Incurable diseases destroy our life and we must change this situation through Yoga.

Shloka (Shiva to Parvati)

इडा गङ्गेति विज्ञेया पिङ्गला यमुना नदी।
मध्ये सरस्वतीं विद्यात्प्रयागादिसमस्तथा॥

English Translation

Ida is called Ganga, Pingla is called Yamuna and Sushumna located in between the two is called Saraswati. The union of three is called Prayag, the Third Eye or Aagya Chakra.

Shloka (Shiva to Parvati)

आदौ साधनमाख्यातं सद्यः प्रत्ययकारकम्।
बद्धपद्मासनो योगी बन्धयेदुड्डियानकम्॥

English Translation

*Oh, Goddess! I am going to tell you the method of doing Sadhna in a way that gives quick result. Firstly, the Yogi will have to sit in Padmasan and lock himself in Uddiyaana bandha.**

*(Uddiyaana Bandha, also called abdominal lock, is employed in Hatha Yoga in particular in the Nauli purification. It involves, after full exhalation and pulling in of abdomen under the rib cage by taking a false inhalation while holding the breath and then releasing the abdomen after a pause. The process is repeated many times before letting the air into the lungs and resuming normal breathing).

The next series of shloka is on the breathing exercises (Pranayama) and their benefits.

Pranayam comprises a set of breathing exercises each serving a specific purpose with each one leaving an impact on the body. Therefore, readers should never attempt these exercises without the guidance of a proper teacher.

Shloka (Shiva to Parvati)

पूरकः कुम्भकश्चैव रेचकश्च तृतीयकः ।
ज्ञातव्यो योगिभिर्नित्यं देहसंशुद्धिहेतवे ॥
पूरकः कुरुते वृद्धिं धातुसाम्यं तथैव च ।
कुम्भके स्तम्भनं कुर्याज्जीवरक्षाविवर्द्धनम् ॥
रेचको हरते पापं कुर्याद्योगपदं व्रजेत् ।
पश्चातसंग्रामवत्तिष्ठेल्लयबन्धं च कारयेत् ॥
कुम्भयेत्सहजं वायुं यथाशक्ति प्रकल्पयेत् ।
रेचयेच्चन्द्रमार्गेण सूर्येणापूरयेत्सुधीः ॥
चन्द्रं पिबति सूर्यश्च सूर्यं पिबति चन्द्रमाः ।

अन्योन्यकालभावेन जीवेदाचन्द्रतारकम् ॥
स्वीयाङ्गे वहते नाडी तन्नाडीरोधनं कुरु।
मुखबन्धममुंचन्वह पवनं जायते युवा॥

English Translation

Pranayam has three actions: Purak, Kumbhak and Rechak. Purak means inhaling to one's optimum capacity. Rechak means to exhale with optimum capacity.

(Kumbhaka is of two types: Internal Kumbhaka: In this, you inhale fully and then hold your breath as long as possible while in external Kumbhaka you exhale forcefully and hold the air out as long as possible).

Purak ensures the nutritional needs of the body for growth and creates the balance among blood, semen and seven minerals in the body. Kumbhaka ensures proper energy flow in the body and strengthens elements of life.

Rechak eliminates the distortions in the body and the mind. Its study makes one a perfect Yogi and achieves a complete balance in his body.

A person should inhale adequately through his right nostril and then do Kumbhaka (holding breath normally before exhaling from the left nostril).

Those who inhale from Moon Nadi (Ida) exhale from the Sun Nadi (Pingla) live longer. This is also called Anulom-Vilom.

Inhale from the active Nadi; close your mouth and do Kumbhaka inside. It makes even old people turn younger.

The following shlokas mention the Sashtmukhi mudra pose that is described in detail in chapter 5 (Flow of Tatva)

Shloka (Shiva to Parvati)

तस्य रूपं गतिः स्वादो मण्डलं लक्षणं त्विदम्।
स वेत्ति मानवो लोके संसर्गादपि मार्गवित्॥
निराशो निष्कलो योगी न किंचिदपि चिन्तयेत्।
वासनामुन्मनां कृत्वा कालं जयति लीलया॥

English Translation

The practitioner of this mudra would easily identify the shape, speed, taste, colour of all five Tatvas; he gains good health and a positive aura for creating good interpersonal communication.

Such a person lives without desires and worries despite living amidst others. He lives like an actor playing a character on the stage and turns into a classic.

Shloka (Shiva to Parvati)

विश्वस्य वेदिकाशक्तिर्नेत्रभ्यां परिदृश्यते।
तत्रस्थं तु मनो यस्य याममात्रं भवेदिह॥
तस्यायुर्वर्द्धते नित्यं घटिकात्रयमानतः।
शिवेनोक्तं पुरा तन्त्रे सिद्धस्य गुणगह्वरे॥
योगीपद्मासनस्थो गुदगतपवनं सन्निरुद्धोर्ध्वमुच्चौस्तं
तस्यापानरन्ध्रे क्रमजितमनिलं प्राणशक्त्या निरुद्धय।

एकीभूतं सुषुम्नाविवरमुपगतं ब्रह्मरन्ध्रे च नीत्वा
निक्षिप्याकाशमार्गे शिवचरणरता यान्ति ते कैपि धन्याः ॥

English Translation

Such a person can see the primal energy that is responsible for running the Srishti (creation) with his eyes. He must focus his mind on this alone.

A practitioner of these methods enhances his life by 1.15 hours per day. This knowledge was given by Shiva to his consort Parvati.

A Yogi in Padmasana uses Moolabandha (Root lock exercise to stop the outflow of his Apan Vayu, one of the five Pranas. The Yogi is able to lift this Prana Vayu through Sushumna to his Sahasrara Chakra (Crown Chakra). This precisely is Dhyana)*

(for details read chapter 5: How to recognise Tatvas)

*(In Sanskrit, Moola Bandha is from Moola meaning Root, base, beginning, foundation, origin or cause; and Bandha meaning bond, fetter, or "catching hold of". Moola Bandha is, "A posture where the body from the anus to the navel is contracted and lifted up and towards the spine". This is qualified in that the actual muscle contracted is neither the sphincter muscle nor the muscle that can stop urination, but the muscle equidistant between the two)

The Root referred to here is the Root of the spine, the pelvic floor or, more precisely, the centre of the pelvic floor, the perineum. The perineum is the muscular body between the anus and the genitals. By slightly contracting the pubococcygeal muscle, which goes from the pubic bone to the tail bone (coccyx), we create an energetic seal that locks Prana into the body and so prevents it from leaking out at the base of the spine. Mula Bandha is said to move Prana into the central channel, called Sushumna, which is the subtle equivalent of the spine.

Shloka (Shiva to Parvati)

एतज्जानाति यो योगी एतत्पठति नित्यशः।
सर्वदुःखविनिर्मुक्तो लभते वांछितं फलम्॥
स्वरज्ञानं भवेद्यस्य लक्ष्मीपदतले भवेत्।
सर्वत्र च शरीरैपिसुखं तस्य सदा भवेत्॥
नाडीत्रयं विजानाति तत्त्वज्ञानं तथैव च।
नैव तेन भवेत्तुल्यं लक्षकोटिरसायनम्॥
एकाक्षरप्रदातारं नाडीभेदविवेचकम्।
पृथिव्यां नास्ति तद्द्रव्यं यद्दत्त्वा चानृणी भवेत्॥

English Translation

A Yogi with the knowledge and who practices it each day is relieved of all his misfortunes and all his wishes are granted at the end of it.

One who practices the science of Swara and adopts it fully has the blessings of Laxmi, the Goddess of wealth. He always enjoys all the bodily pleasures.

One who acquires the proper knowledge of three Nadis and all five Tatvas in equal measure, becomes omniscient. All herbs, medicines and chemicals together fail to match his self-healing powers. He does not need any of these as with his knowledge of five Tatva and three Nadis, he can even defeat death.

If a Yogi who has acquired the knowledge of all the above, shares a small part of it with you, you should consider yourself as the richest person on the earth. You will always remain indebted to him.

Below is a few Do-it-yourself tricks (Teacher/ Guru not required) that should be practised each day to see you succeed in whatever you do, raise your self-confidence and enjoy good health:

1. After waking up check the active Nadi. If it is left one-Ida–turn your face in the South or West direction. If your Pingla is at work then turn the face to north or east. Touch the side of the face on the side of your Nadi with the palm of the same side hand.

2. While doing the above exercise for the right Nadi, focus your mind on Sun and feel the sun rays enter your heart and energize the body. For the left Nadi, focus your mind on Moon and feel its benign light enter your heart and pour the elixir of life in.

3. Thereafter, touch the floor with the hand on the side of your active Nadi and put the same side foot down.

Tips for The Daily Routine

1. Always defecate with the right Nadi in active mode and urinate with the left on.
2. Eat food in the right Nadi time and lie down on the left side of the body for 10-15 minutes afterwards.
3. Drink water when the left Nadi is active.
4. Sleep when the right Nadi is active and wake up with the left one.

Tips For Good Results In Daily Tasks

1. While leaving for work always take the foot on the side of active Nadi out.
2. The right Nadi active time is better for entering someone's house.
3. Addressing public meeting or studying gets the best results if done in the flow time of left Nadi.
4. Meditation, auspicious tasks, house warming etc. should be started when the left Nadi is active.
5. Long journeys should be started when the left Nadi is active and smaller trips when the right one is active.
6. When the left Nadi is active in the day and right in the night it is considered an ideal situation from the point of view of health, intellect and spiritualism.

RECAP

- Inhalation is accompanied by the sound Hun and exhalation by Sah.
- During Dhyana the breathing becomes very slow and at this stage, one can experience the 'Hansa' sound. If we learn to hear the sound of air as we breathe out till we start breathing in it is Hans: its reverse – from inhalation to start of exhalation – would turn out to be Soham.
- During Sushmna's activity, when Ida and Pingla meet, the air coming in and going out also meet at one point. This point is the union of Hun and Sah.
- Hun symbolizes Shiva and Sah Shakti.
- Akash Tatva flows in Sushumna and the length of the breath is four fingers and therefore the shortest. On getting into meditation at this stage, gradually the length shortens further.

❑❑❑

PART II-THE MIND

10

CHAPTER

You Can Control The World

By now, we have come to know of many secrets of the breath through Swara. The importance of breath for life is supreme. Do you agree? May be you do or do not. Just think of it: who said 'yes' or 'no' to this question? Of course, it is your mind. This means besides breath, the mind is also important for us as it is responsible for our thoughts. As you read this, it is your mind that's active. Surprisingly, the Swara Shastra has no mention of the mind even as it deals extensively with the parallel phenomenon of breathing. Our state of mind has a direct impact on our breathing. Therefore, a discussion on the breath is incomplete without the topic of mind.

The breath is the physical form of mind. The state of one's mind impacts the speed of breathing. All this merits the study of the mind.

All religions and cultures believe that no meaningful study can be done without knowing your mind. This is not only true about spiritualism but even in routine life. The mind is behind all feelings of happiness, grief, bliss, ecstasy etc. What is the mind? How is it so powerful that it can drive us in any direction? Are your mind and you two different entities? Am I the same as my mind?

The understanding of the mind is the key to embarking on the path of spirituality. The mind is like a lock behind which is the real you. Therefore, if you are able to find the keys to this lock, your quest for everything else ends. To get to the key, therefore, it is important to study the lock. You will end up realising that it is a unique lock that hides its key within.

We all are in pursuit of happiness that comes from money, fame, sex, success etc. All humans go after material things for happiness. However, our hot pursuit ends as soon as we get our desire fulfilled. We want money to build a house or buy luxuries and essential stuff; a spouse to live happily with her/him. Interestingly, the same things stop looking attractive after we acquire them. Very soon, we start the next chase for happiness.

Why is happiness ephemeral? The problem is that while happiness is an internal reaction our senses make us believe it lay outside us. We find ourselves attracted to things and situations to the extent that we begin to see happiness in the material world. The reality is that no material thing can give us eternal happiness and satiate our desires for blissfulness. We are looking for happiness in the wrong place. How can we get something that doesn't exist? As they say, money can literally buy you everything but peace, happiness and love; it can make the world look comfortable, attractive and colourful exactly like an artificial flower with no fragrance.

Only a rich man, who possesses all that the poor aspires for and dreams of, can explain how hollow and unhappy he feels from inside. However, a person without means can never appreciate it until he too experiences the possessions. If money could buy happiness, all the rich and resourceful people would be the happiest in the world. A peep into the lives of the rich illustrates this. A penniless person lives on hope and dreams of striking gold someday.

However, a rich and unhappy person does not even have hope. A poor person can barely empathise with him going through suffocation, incompleteness and helplessness. The fact is the rich are also in pursuit of eternal happiness. Many westerners abandon their comfortable lifestyles and material possessions to come to a poorer country like India in search of happiness and peace. They may have a good reason to do so.

Ask a person; is he always happy and the answer invariably would be nobody under the sun has ever achieved total happiness. Humans are breaking new frontiers in science; have reached Moon and yet they cannot find a recipe for happiness. So, should we assume that life is full of miseries only or maybe it is a mixed bag? Look at another possibility: maybe science is yet to explore and find a formula for eternal happiness.

According to science, behind every happening there is a cause and it is called the cause and effect phenomenon. According to this, there has to be a cause for the miseries of humans. If we can identify the cause, it is possible to find the cure. This was Gautam Buddha's basic philosophy. He asked humans to search for the cause behind their misery and then cure it.

This raises another question: where does one experience happiness or misery? Take the case of you feeling good after meeting someone. Maybe while shaking hands, you told him, "Pleasure meeting you". Where does this pleasure happen? It is inside you!

The feeling of happiness, sadness or misery is an internal process and yet we look for their causes outside. Looking out is an alibi. In fact, we are the creators of our happiness and misery. If my child tops in the class, I am happy; if the neighbour's child gets higher marks than him, I feel upset. It is not the examination but my attachment to my son that is the real cause of my feelings.

The feeling of happiness or sadness does not come as bodily pain or fever. Does an injured foot tell you that it is in pain? This feeling is conveyed by our mind. It means all our reactions of pain, happiness, pleasure etc. are conveyed by the mind from inside. When the feelings of happiness and sadness come from inside, the cause of the same cannot exist outside. Also, when we have found the cause for the pain, it is not beyond our reach to find the antidote.

Since we are unaware of the power of our mind, including healing, we are unable to use it. The mind is not an ordinary entity. It cannot be easily understood; it is omnipotent. It moves at a speed that exceeds that of the light. Normally we are subservient to the mind but if we can manage to turn around the game and learn to control it, our search for everything will end. The mind can make us achieve both in the spiritual and the material world.

There is an interesting story of a Master and his servant that explains the nuances of our relationship with the mind. Each morning, the master left home for work. In the evening, on return, he handed over all his earnings to the servant, who, in turn, kept it in a safe place. This continued for many years and the house was full of goodies.

One day when the master returned, he found the servant at the door. The boy took the stuff from the master and told him curtly that as the house was full there was no place for him inside. The servant wanted to throw out some stuff to make a place for the master.

The master didn't want to throw things bought with his hard-earned money. He preferred to stay put outside than dispose of things. From that day, he slept under the open sky and kept bringing goodies. This again continued for a long time. Gradually the servant realised that his master cared more about material things than himself. He also understood that the house and the things inside were in his possession and he felt powerful.

His ambitions soared; he visualized himself as the owner of the house. He hit upon a plan. He disposed of some of the goods to raise money for expanding the house. He shifted its main door towards the courtyard.

The first day the master returned he didn't notice the change; as usual, handed his earnings to the servant and settled outside. That day he was shocked by the servant's angry voice, "Can't you see I am repairing the house? After all, it is my responsibility to take care of everything". He directed the master to move beyond the courtyard on to the road.

The master was helpless due to his addiction to hoarding. He mechanically worked all day and ended up by the roadside in the night; his servant lived a good life inside the house.

His obsession had turned him away from reality. He forgot that the man ordering him to stay outside was his servant. His addiction was getting better of him. The Master was living on the road while the servant enjoyed a good life, ate good food and became strong. The Master lost his stature and authority.

However, the servant was always haunted by fear what if the master remembered the reality, asked him to rearrange stuff and make a place for him inside. He could even get fired. The wily servant hit upon another plan: he would keep the master busy with chores so that he had no time to even think. The Master was not allowed to even take rest and not given time to reflect.

In this allegory, the owner of the house is you and the servant is your mind. The material possession, the owner hands over to his servant daily, is your memories.

Whatever you see, hear, feel or experience in the day gets deposited as memory in your mind. It is the stock of memories that makes your mind grow and become powerful enough to control you. Your mind uses your memories to send you thoughts and ideas to keep you occupied. In short, you create a mind; empower it and ultimately it rules you.

The mind becomes the master and keeps sending us on errands through our thoughts. It does not allow us to pause and take rest. It becomes too powerful for us to tackle it and we always end up following it. In case we can fulfil its desires, it pats and makes us feel happy for a while. If we fail, it reprimands and makes us feel miserable. We keep serving the mind all our life.

If we decide to fight the Mind, we will be the losers. The mind is so powerful that the fight would look like a match between a WWF wrestler and an emaciated person.

What are the ways to tame the mind?

Always remember, we are speaking about taming the mind and not destroying it. It is not our enemy. Some people try to destroy the mind but never succeed and end up feeling miserable.

What is the best approach to deal with as powerful an entity as the mind? We would be wasting time and effort in trying to destroy it. The best situation is when we are able to gain control over it. This way we can be the owner of the mind and use it. How can this be achieved?

The conscious mind being so powerful, it will never allow us to gain control over it. It can only be done when it is unconscious. This process can be done through Dhyana in which our breath plays a key role. Before we move to the study of Dhyana, we must know more about the mind.

The Mind

Where is the mind located inside our body? How was it created? Most of us think that we are the mind. So, the feeling of being too must be coming from the mind. This is a myth perpetuated by our ignorance. In case, you become unconscious, your mind will not work and yet you continue to exist. So, how do you explain this? When you sleep you lose touch with your mind and yet you are there. This proves that you and your mind are different.

However, it is difficult to tell the mind from our being and in our thinking, the two are entwined. Our existence is pure consciousness (Shuddha Chetna); the mind gives us the feeling of our existence. Our mind experiences images and sounds every day and makes them available to us as and when we need these. At the time of the birth, the child has no idea of life. The memory of previous births lies deep in his consciousness and he is not aware of it.

With each passing day, the child picks knowledge of images – of his parents and other members of his family. He senses that a particular face comes to his rescue whenever he feels hungry. These faces communicate through sound. The mother would say, "See, who has come: your daddy?" or "Are you feeling hungry, shall I feed you?" His mind registers the mother's face as an image and her speech as sound. Later when someone utters the same words, the child begins to look for the corresponding image. Gradually the memories keep growing and so does the mind.

When he becomes aware, he records everything that he hears, sees, tastes, smells or feels through touch as memory. At this stage, the development of mind, intellect, consciousness and ego starts. The mind is part of Antahkarana* that is always linked to intellect and Chitta. Like the data saved in our mobile phone, whatever our senses perceive gets stored as memory in our mind.

*(In Hindu Philosophy the Antahkarana is a Sanskrit word, meaning ("the inner cause or internal organ"). It comprises four parts:

1. Manas (mind) – controls willpower or resolution
2. Buddhi (intellect) – controls decision-making

3. Chitta (memory)–deals with remembering and forgetting

4. Ahenkar (ego) – identifies the Atman(self) with the body as 'I'

As a child grows, memories keep flooding his mind. Since all this information is stored either as a sound or image, the mind flashes the image whenever someone speaks the corresponding sound (memory) and he can visualize it. Likewise, if we see an image, the memory of which is there, the mind flashes its name to us. The mind creates ideas for us on the basis of memory. The mind, however, will not be able to help us with things, images, sounds and feelings (by touch) that we are encountering for the first time. This is quite significant.

For example, if you are told the word, Rose, immediately its shape, smell, colour and all that you know about it will flash in your mind. Will it ring a bell in your mind if you hear the word 'Bruser'? Your mind may become curious to know about this word. Since there is no memory about 'Bruser' the mind will be clueless. I am sure you must not be even curious about this word before reading it here.

'Bruser' is the Rose in the Danish language which is spoken in Denmark and other parts of Europe. Since your mind has registered this new sound and knowledge, next time you come across it, the image of a rose will flash in your mind. Our mind gives different names to the same thing for convenience. This is important for comprehension and communication. However, giving two or more names to one object for the sake of better understanding and proper communication is not the same as taking the same object as two different entities.

Let's understand this easily and practically. Look around the room where you are sitting: there are things like the chair, table, windows, couch, flower vase etc. All these things come from the earth. Like the table, chair and windows come from a tree and we have given them different names. This is done mainly for the sake of understanding while the fact is all these are wood that comes out of Earth.

Similarly, all that we see around us – from a car to a toy – has originated from Earth. Each one has a different shape and we have given them different names.

However, the fact is that each one is destined to merge with the earth sooner or later. At this stage, you may find it hard to believe that everything in the world comprises five Tatva that are shaped differently to create the world.

Conscious and Unconscious Mind

Our mind starts with using five elements (Tatva): earth, water, fire, air and space with different and multiple names. Since the mind does not have the capacity to store all these names in one place, it is bifurcated into Chetan Man (conscious mind with awareness) and Achetan Man (unconscious mind). The dichotomy is confusing. The mind that we know is the conscious mind. We do not realise that the real force behind the mind is a much more powerful unconscious mind.

The example of a large ice slab dipped in water can explain the relationship between two levels of the mind. One can clearly see the part of the ice slab above the water surface and yet would have no idea about the size and shape of the submerged portion. The submerged part is nine times larger. Similarly, the unconscious mind is nine times powerful than the conscious mind. The mind as we know stores very little information; the bulk of it is transferred to the unconscious mind. The conscious mind follows intellect while the unconscious is unbridled and autonomous. Our lives are controlled by our unconscious mind. It bypasses the intellect and the overt mind to make us follow it.

Some Psychologists believe there are three minds – conscious, subconscious and unconscious. However, without getting into that debate, in this book, we take it that the subconscious mind (as defined by psychologists) is a part of the unconscious mind.

Psychologists have drawn differences between the two minds and their respective properties. These are enumerated in the table below:

Conscious Mind	Unconscious Mind
1. It works only when we are awake	It functions round the clock even while we are asleep
2. It seeks the help of intellect	Functions independently; doesn't need help
3. It executes a task	It organizes and plans a task

4. It understands logic	It doesn't go by logic; it functions arbitrarily and goes by whims
5. It functions as a filter for passing information to the unconscious mind; selects information for passing on	It has an unlimited stock of information and no filter; can cobble a dream out of any combination of memories. It's seamless
6. It has limited power	Its energy and power are unlimited
7. It uses discretion for time and place	It has no respect for values and scant regard for time and place
8. It has to learn	It doesn't need to learn: it makes its own permutations and combinations of the information supplied by the overt mind to improvise things
9. It works in isolation	It's into creative functioning
10. It consults intellect and uses discretion	It's rudderless; has no link with intellect whatsoever
11. It fixes a target	It involves a target

12. It's the master. However, on lowering its guard it becomes subservient to the unconscious mind	It's the servant who overpowers the master (conscious mind) and rules over him
13. It's Aladdin (who owns a magical lamp)	It's the genie who comes out of Aladdin's lamp
14. It has limited memory. It is dependent on the unconscious mind for refreshing its memory.	It has unlimited information. It never loses information, handles any request for information from the conscious mind arbitrarily.

From a long list, these are the key differences between the two minds. In fact, 90 per cent of our routine tasks like feeling hungry, thirsty, sleeping and waking up etc. are regulated by the unconscious mind.

Both these minds have their respective set of tasks to perform. While speaking with others, we gesticulate and wear facial expression. Both are involuntary actions that we cannot pre-mediate. Nobody has taught us gesticulation and making expressions. If something appeals to our conscious mind, it immediately approaches the unconscious mind. At this stage, the unconscious mind takes charge and it makes us gesticulate and give an expression.

However, while gesticulating, if your mind focuses on the hand, you can control the action. The action of stopping the hand is directed by the conscious mind.

This is what is called living consciously. However, we are generally running around in life in an auto mode as all our routine actions are fed in the unconscious mind and everything goes on without our conscious mind having to bother. The unconscious mind decides how we should react to a situation based on the pre-fed information.

Similarly, something comes in front of our eyes, we close these without thinking. When someone abuses us, our reaction is already fed in the unconscious mind. So the reaction will be as per the feeding. We quickly respond to an insulting remark. In case we can go to our conscious mind even for a split second, we will react mindfully.

This is bound to be helpful to us. Often the unconscious mind numbs our conscious mind.

The unconscious mind has premeditated impressions and it keeps practising the same. So within seconds of a situation, it is ready with a response and we follow it like puppets. We get angry at someone hurling invectives on us; the unconscious mind is ready in no time with a reaction that is based on our first encounter with a similar situation earlier.

The unconscious mind works on the basis of estimated proof. Take the case of siblings of whom the older boy often bullied his brother. Your unconscious mind has registered the behaviour of the older child. Later on, one day the younger one comes crying and complains that his brother has hit him. You immediately trust him and scold the older boy.

However, the fact is that on that day, the younger child had played a smart game of blaming his brother for no apparent reason. Your reaction was based on the first impression of the boys' behaviour. You ended up scolding the older boy because your unconscious mind has already given you an estimated proof in the form of the first memory about the older one.

Our unconscious mind generates reactions based on assumptions made from limited information. Such perceptions are wrong and often harmful. In case we take a deep breath before reacting to a particular situation, our conscious mind will use intellect to analyse it properly and our reaction will be appropriate.

Fear and anger are also created by our unconscious mind. Besides, it is wrong to believe that others make us angry. Take for instance this case: you are driving when a cycle rickshaw hits your car. Your anger knows no bounds; you come out of the car and shout at the rickshaw puller. Again your car is hit. This time after coming out of your car you see a policeman with a stick in his hand. Will you react the same way? Definitely not! This time yours' is a thoughtful reaction.

The fear also works on similar lines. While passing through a jungle on a dark night, you feel someone, possibly a ghost is following you. Those who believe in ghosts will feel more scared and can hear their footsteps. As fear grows in their minds, they take their own footsteps for that of the Ghost. In case he dares to look behind he would surely see a ghost. Here, the unconscious mind is playing games. In case one can manage to take a deep breath before reacting, our conscious mind will step in and help us stay calm.

When the conscious mind is not alert to the surroundings, the unconscious mind takes charge in no time. It keeps repeating reactions and this makes us unknowingly pick good and bad habits. When something goes deeper into our unconscious mind, the habit developed thereby never goes away. The conscious mind wants to change but yields in front of the unconscious mind that has enormous powers. However, if one can manage the mammoth of an unconscious mind and use its powers through willpower, nothing is impossible.

Why are we not able to use the power of the unconscious mind? Let's analyse the reasons for this.

The conscious mind acts as a filter; it can stop the flow of information or alter it before sending it to the unconscious mind. This is the biggest strength of the conscious mind. We must remember the unconscious mind can only get information fed to it. The conscious mind, therefore, can pass only the relevant information and block the rest. The unconscious mind has no power to change this. However, most of us are not aware of this unique power of the conscious mind.

We learn and practice a skill through our conscious mind. As our learning is complete, the unconscious mind takes charge and for the rest of our lives, it is the latter that directs us in that task. The conscious mind has no power to delete the information it is fed; it can only add to what it has sent to the unconscious mind. You must have heard people saying, "I tried hard; my mind does not support my effort". In this case, the mind that's trying hard is the conscious one and the one not helping is the unconscious mind. The conscious mind has weak willpower.

For example, when we are learning to swim or drive, we use our conscious mind. While training, our mind is always on high alert and receives instructions carefully. Once you have learned it, you will notice that both driving and swimming happen automatically, without application of mind. In reality, you are not in auto mode. During the training, our conscious mind had been passing all the information to the unconscious mind and afterwards the latter uses the same information to make us do that task effortlessly. Similarly, even in deep sleep, our hand rises to squat a mosquito that bites us. In sleep, our conscious mind is resting but the unconscious mind is active.

The conscious mind's job is to remain alert and collect all information about a task. It filters the information and passes the relevant bit to the unconscious mind.

Thereafter the unconscious mind makes this information available to the conscious mind whenever required. This happens with super speed unmatched by even a supercomputer. Think of something and the unconscious mind will bring you all the relevant information about it. However, the same power of the unconscious mind never allows us to remain calm.

As the mind is trying to concentrate; the unconscious mind disturbs it by sending messages and pushes it to another task. Unless the work is significant or urgent we too toe the line of the unconscious mind. In such a situation we say, 'my mind isn't working', and give up.

The conscious mind is like a Rishi Vishwamitra (sage) who is into his Tapasya (prayer); the unconscious mind is like Indra (King of heavens), who wants to break the sage's dhyana either by desecrating the holy fire lit in front of him or by sending Menka, the most beautiful of Apsaras in heaven, to lure him into lust and love, and get distracted. How can one rein in the unconscious mind; what happens if we are able to overpower it?

Strong Willpower

We know that the conscious mind filters information before sending it to the unconscious mind. In this, the conscious mind consults the intellect that follows logic and weighs the pros and cons of a situation. Therefore, many a time, the conscious mind likes to do something but it is rejected by the intellect that works on the basis of pragmatism. The intellect dismisses the idea by saying it is not possible. In that case, the information will not go to the unconscious mind. Had this information reached the unconscious mind it would have made it possible.

This is because the unconscious mind does not work based on logic. Therefore, we can never achieve something stupendous without the help of the unconscious mind.

Take the case of you trying to solve a mathematical problem. Your intellect works on it and yet you cannot solve it. Ultimately you keep the book aside and give up. Since the mind has not been able to resolve it, it does not send the question to the unconscious mind. However, if sometimes, after giving up suddenly a solution will click inside your mind. It is because after you giving up the effort to solve it and staying calm, the question has somehow reached the unconscious mind. At this you may quip, "I just got an idea!"

This is how this happened: when your intellect gives in and you close the chapter, the unconscious mind keeps trying to resolve the question. As soon as it does, it sends it to the conscious mind and we believe the idea has suddenly come to us. This is the power of the unconscious mind. There is always a force behind what all happens on the earth; nothing happens on its own.

Sometimes we can see this force and the other time it is latent.

You must have already heard about the Law of Attraction that says whatever we think continuously starts occurring in our real-life however, many people are not able to achieve much through this Law of Attraction. The main reason behind this is that their unconscious mind does not support the conscious mind.

The trick is if we can join the conscious and unconscious minds through our willpower, nothing will ever be impossible. The conscious mind that we mostly use is just 10 per cent and it is subservient to the 90 per cent more powerful unconscious mind. Also, we have no power to control the unconscious mind nor does it have any link with intellect. It is not into doing right or wrong things. It works arbitrarily. However, the reality is that we are the owners of our unconscious minds too. Just think of the possibilities in case we can connect the two minds and become their rightful owner! The high intellect is born from the joining of the two minds.

The connection between the conscious and unconscious mind happens in three situations:

1. When the conscious mind is studying, practising or learning something with deep interest;
2. Do-or-die situation for us.
3. When the conscious mind is enjoying itself or having a great experience.

In these situations, the two minds pool their energy. At this stage, the unconscious mind does not disturb the conscious mind; instead, it helps it to concentrate.

Together they can make mountains move. The two minds also connect during storytelling. Here is a real-life story to illustrate all this:

Willpower & The Law of Attraction

This is the story of a blind woman who appeared on an Indian Television reality show. This Sikh woman from a village in Punjab brandished swords in her hands and wore a cap-like contraption on her head. The cap had iron chains with spiked metal balls at their end. These balls would move in a circular motion with the help of a tool. She was pitted against four rivals – able-bodied men on the show.

The audiences were in for the biggest surprise of their lives. They were wondering how a visionless woman would fight four normal well-built men. As the competition started, she was all over the place; moving like a whirlwind using her swords and the pendulum-type spiked balls with the help of her head. Soon swords fell of the hands of the four men. They gave up and jumped out. She had developed a sense of tracking her rivals through their foot movement.

Her story is inspiring. She had lost vision during her pregnancy. Unfortunately, her husband passed away soon. She became destitute and took shelter in a Gurudwara where a Nihang priest noticed her. He wondered how a blind woman would take care of her child all alone. Her child was born in the Gurudwara. The same priest noticed one thing about her: she always kept the child close to her chest. When he began to crawl, she would keep tabs on him by keeping her mind focused on the sound of his hands and feet. The Nihang was impressed and decided to take her under his wings.

The priest, who was a brilliant sword fighter, had found his understudy. He was banking on her special ability to recognise even the feeblest of the sounds accurately and started her training. With her strong willpower, the woman was coming up as a goodswords-woman. She often woke up in the middle of the night for practice.

On that TV show, the world saw the strength of the human spirit and willpower.

Let's analyse how the sword woman's mind worked all through. After losing her eyesight, she had realised the irrelevance of material possessions. The conscious mind is often distracted by what our eyes see and ears hear. The information that she has to lead her life without eyesight was deposited in her unconscious mind. Now, her conscious mind was focused on a singular thought: how to bring up her child. Since she faced a dire situation, the only message her conscious mind sent to her unconscious mind was how would I spend the rest of my life and take care of my child. The unconscious mind began working relentlessly to give replies to her questions. This woman had no choice. In fact, alternatives deflect your attention and do not permit you to focus. In case one is faced with no options in a dire situation, one gets equipped with strong will power.

Husband's death plunged her into grief and she lost interest in the world. Grief also united her two minds. This is because a grieving person's conscious mind stops and the unconscious mind takes over. In the Gurudwara, her mind was preoccupied with the worry about her yet to be born child. This message had gone to the unconscious mind. Her mind must always be conveying to her that she has no choice but to take care of her child under all circumstances. With each passing day, her willpower became stronger; suddenly nothing was impossible for her. The energy of her unconscious mind helped her learn the once impossible sword fighting and focus on her child. She became good at identifying targets by the sound of their movement. Her unconscious mind generated the idea that martial arts would enable her to raise her child and brace for life.

Some of you may be wondering why we are not able to do what that woman did. She didn't set out with a big and dramatic target like appearing on TV for herself. She began with the simple target of learning and practised rigorously and with determination. One day, the big target literally walked to her.

All successful people have a common trait: they focus on a specific area. In real life, there are no overnight rags to riches stories. Behind the success of every person is the saga of hard work and sacrifice. For achieving success, one's conscious mind should be focused. You should be very sure of it; in case there are questions and doubts about it in your mind, it will never happen. There should not be even a single negative thought about it in your mind. You have to think as I can do it and I shall do it come what may. That way success is certain. If you can generate such a positive thought, you will never face failure. This is how the Law of Attraction works.

To begin with, one should never have a big target in what would love to do. Enjoy the process and keep practising. When the conscious mind shows determination to do a task, the unconscious mind supplies it with the required information. The conscious mind just has to decide and fix a target and the unconscious mind will pursue it to the end. The unconscious mind has an amazing capacity to use other's unconscious mind to achieve the target.

The unconscious mind has another layer called collective unconsciousness. All collective unconscious minds are akin to the internet and can pass messages. When required, the unconscious mind can send messages to the unconscious mind of others. The linkage between two layers of unconscious minds will be dealt with in the next chapter.

We must also remember that options bar our determination and willpower. To begin with, the mental exercise for becoming successful, one must delete all options and focus on just one way. Options split our mind energy in various directions; when we focus on just one thing, all mind energy works on it and everything starts falling in place.

The blind woman's heroism tells us about the power of the unconscious mind. In real terms, this energy is vast; it cannot be realised with the science of psychology. It can be felt only through spiritual practices. At the end of imparting knowledge to Arjuna in the middle of the Mahabharata war, Krishna asks him to go to his Guru Bhishma who was on his death bed. Bhishma was known for his pledge and will power. Only a man with strong willpower can live up to his pledge. Krishna had sent Arjuna to Bhishma to gain knowledge about willpower. Without willpower, Krishna knew Arjuna would not be able to follow the lessons that he has just imparted to him (Bhagwat Gita).

Most of us pray to seek favours. Sometimes the prayers are answered while most of the times these are not. Have you ever thought about why some prayers are answered and some not? The story below will make you understand this.

Once upon a time, there was a businessman who worshipped Lord Ganesha. Each morning, he prayed to the deity and asked him to keep his family safe and happy. One day he had an important meeting to attend to. The outcome of the meeting was crucial for his business. That day he prayed, "O Ganapati Bappa, keep me and my family safe and happy and favour me by making my meeting successful".

Soon he left for the airport to catch his flight. His car broke down on the way. The businessman scolded his driver for not taking care of the vehicle. Eventually, he missed his flight and also the meeting.

He was upset the whole day. He was also disturbed because he felt the Lord didn't hear his prayer. He took out his anger on his employees in the office. In the evening, when he was at home, he switched on the television. What he saw sent a chill down his spine. The plane he had missed had crashed. He rushed to the temple inside his home and thanked Ganesha for saving his life.

He had been praying to Ganesha for years for his and his family's safety. This prayer had settled deep down in his unconscious mind and created strong willpower. The other prayer – for the success of the meeting – was said that day and had not percolated to his unconscious mind. They say a prayer said with emotions and conviction is always answered.

Psychology also recognises the unlimited magic of willpower and that it emerges from the unconscious mind.

RECAP

- A human being pursues happiness in everything be it money, fame, sex, career etc. He runs after these just to become happy. The moment he gets these, his happiness evaporates and he starts pursuing other things.

- Happiness is an internal process while we keep looking for it outside. Our senses divert us to happiness outside.

- In the world outside us, there is nothing that can give long lasting happiness. If material pursuits could give all the happiness, the rich would be the happiest. The fact is that even the rich and powerful are in search of happiness.

- Many mix one's being with his mind. It is not true. If it is so how can we continue to exist while the mind doesn't exist under anaesthesia?

- Even in sleep, we do exist but our mind ceases to exist. So, the two are different entities.

- What we call the mind, is the conscious mind. However, there is unconscious mind behind it; nine times more powerful than the former. Most of our ideas emerge from the unconscious mind.

- Our mind throws up hundreds of ideas simultaneously. So many ideas scatter the energy of the mind and weaken the power of ideas. The energy of a single idea can move mountains.

❑❑❑

11

CHAPTER

Seven Levels of Mind

Science does not recognise the soul, Atma. Till some time ago, it didn't even recognise the concept of the Mind. However, today science defines the mind as consciousness, peculiar to humans. Mind that is consciousness, keeps humans alive and makes them understand their surroundings. The knowledge humans acquire through the mind is labelled as intellect or the power of thoughts. For science, the human being is just a body and mind. The latter is a bundle of memories located inside the brain, something like the software in a computer.

Owing to its limitations, science fails to explain many phenomena. For example, it has no explanation for the sudden death of a healthy person. Though doctors can find out the cause of his death through post mortem examination yet they fail to give answers to many questions that arise from it. In the same way, we can get our blood examined in a pathological laboratory.

Physicians can point out issues with it that impact our health and prescribe medicines for cure. However, the science that has produced test-tube baby, is yet to discover the formula for making artificial blood.

The human body and all its parts are made of seven Dhatus* (tissues).

* Dhatu is a Sanskrit word meaning layer or stratum, constituent part or ingredient.

All parts of our body are made of seven fundamental Dhatu or their mix. These seven Dhatus are:

1. Rasa Dhatu (Lymph)
2. Rakta Dhatu (Blood)
3. Mamsa Dhatu (Muscle)
4. Medha Dhatu (Fat)
5. Asthi Dhatu (Bone)
6. Majja Dhatu (Bone marrow)
7. Shukra Dhatu (Semen)

These Dhatu are manufactured by five subtle elements or Tatva– Jal (Water) and Vayu (Air), Aakash (Space), Prithvi (Earth), and Agni (Fire). Dhatu is not a mineral available outside; it is manufactured inside the body.

These are created by consciousness and mind power as per a prefixed blueprint. Each animal and plant species acquires characteristics that are stored in its seed in the form of information. Science calls it genetic code. And we have to remember that like all other things, science has accepted it only after verification.

Though science has come to accept the concept of Mind; it is yet to do the same with Chetna (Consciousness). Chetna is a power that differentiates the living and the dead. Do you believe you are a body with a brain that has memory inside to run the system?

Or you feel your existence is more than just your body and mind?

If you are your body, then your body should feel happy when you do. It is just the reverse. For example, a body injury gives us pain that is conveyed by our mind. The mind is there to make us feel it. Who feels the pain or in other cases pleasure?

Let's assume you are just a body that runs as per the stock of memories or the mind stored in your brain. We already know that as per science the consciousness is located in the mind and the latter is a bundle of memories. In case all your memories get erased in an accident, you do not cease to exist. Sometimes people lose their memory and yet they continue to exist. This means there is more than the brain and memory in the body that makes us feel our existence. It surely cannot be the mind because, after the loss of memory, it does not exist. So what makes you experience your existence even without the memory?

In the light of what science tells us about the location of the mind, have you ever wondered why people from different cultures and countries always place their hand on their hearts while saying tender and emotional lines like, "I love you", and not on their head? Even while making a promise or a pledge, we follow the same gesture and it is a universal behaviour. In India, we often thump our chest to say, "This is my word. I am taking responsibility". If we are only body then we could say such things by just thumping any part of our body may be a thigh, stomach or back etc. Have you ever thought why all humans touch their hearts when to express emotions?

Language, Expression and Silence

We generally tend to believe that thoughts arise from the mind. However, these thoughts have an origin. The seed of emotion rests near our hearts, in Anahat Chakra (Heart Chakra). This is why we have the feeling of our existence closer to the heart.

Our thoughts are gross and lurid while the emotions are subtle. We are able to see the thoughts on the radius of a circle yet not its epicentre, the location of the seed of the emotion. This makes us believe that our feelings emanate from the mind. It is a major and the most common mistake we make.

Emotions are innate to humans; nobody teaches you how to feel happy, scared, loved, angry, upset, hungry etc. When you feel scared, something happens close to your heart; it skips a beat. The feelings of love, hate, pity, mercy etc. all emanate from the same area. Does something tickle in your head whenever you feel happy or sad? No, it is always the heart that reacts. We would say, "My heartfelt thanks", and never "my brain-felt or mind-felt thank you!"

Emotions are always pure though the language to express these could be artificial. At times, the language can be totally opposite of your feeling. For example, you always praise your boss though you may not like him. As you interact with him, your heart has hate for him but you always speak reverentially to him. You cannot change or manipulate the feeling while you can manipulate your language.

It was some 5,000 years ago that humans invented the language to fulfil their need to communicate effectively.

Since human history dates back to one hundred thousand years it means for 95,000 years, they lived without language skills. Back then they didn't have a language to express themselves yet their innate emotions of love, hate, anger, pity were the same as it is of today's humans.

Let's go back to the era when man created language and the script. There was no university or a school to make him learn it. Just think of how did he get the idea of creating the language? He must have used the basic sounds coming naturally to him to lay the foundation of language. All sounds come from the region between the throat to the tip of the tongue. Devnagri, Sanskrit all have basic sounds as consonants and alphabets. At this stage, the human race was closest to consciousness and in this stage, it had the highest level of intellect that helped it create the language.

Today when due to the language and the script, learning has become easier, humans are not able to invent a new language or script. It is because this is not an easy task. The idea of creating a language came from the sound of man's inner silence. However, things started floundering from this point. The language was created to communicate with fellow humans and not with ourselves. Humans have practised this distortion for too long and given up the decorum of observing inner silence. This habit refuses to go.

The habit of talking to ourselves deprives us of silence. The words debar us from reaching pure Bhava (Emotions) that we need to use to communicate with ourselves. Silence is the way to reach Bhava while we are stuck in language. Silence is a great communicator. Language is 100 per cent effective only if it is matching with Bhava.

The ancient man used language only when he needed it. In that situation, his Bhava (Emotions), language, expression and body language were completely synchronised. Gradually, he became greedy and fearful and these habits made him clever and he started mixing the language with Bhava (Emotions).

Today the language created to express man's emotions is being used for camouflaging the same.

Humans have brought themselves into a situation where a mismatch between emotions and language is considered politeness. For example, a wife asks her husband, "How do I look?"

Husband: "Gorgeous!"

While the reality may be the wife's inner emotion is, "Are you having an affair?"

The husband's real feeling is, "You always looked the same: why trouble me today".

Another situation: A woman wants to have sex when the man she meets. Will she be able to tell him honestly? She may praise him and make suggestive comments.

Since the Bhava and language do not match, the impact is not felt.

A study in the USA says that in verbal communication only 2 per cent of the message is conveyed and the rest is done through body language and vibes.

We always talk to ourselves in the same language that we use for thinking, reading or listening to others. Mostly we do not listen to others. During a 'conversation' we are either waiting for the speaker to finish or for our turn to speak. Instead of listening to him, we are judging him.

That clearly means no communication is happening. Unfortunately, we consider it a conversation.

Our mind is never silent; it keeps speaking to itself while we believe this is the process of thought creation. Creation of a thought is a subtle inner process and is unrelated to the language. A thought arises from consciousness and we use language to convey it. It is evident the way the ancient man had got the idea of language for the first time through silence. It is always in silence that humans get in touch with their pure consciousness. This is the reason why original ideas come only through inner silence.

Are we silent even when we are not speaking to someone? In reality, we keep speaking with ourselves. It is like a madman's soliloquy; the difference is the madman is loud and we do not use our voice. Barring conversations with others, we must learn to keep silent. Worrying never helps; original ideas including a solution to a problem will come to you only in silence. The emergence of an idea is a sudden process. Language is for the use of the brain and that is the reason expression through language can be manipulated. Communication with one's inner-self or the Almighty, therefore, should always be held through pure emotions, Bhava.

During a ceremonial prayer, a pandit or a purohit (Hindu priest) instructs you to invoke Gods through Bhava. Interestingly, he chants prayers loudly and yet insists on you creating emotions while making a symbolic offering to the deity. Ask him how Bhava is created and he would feel offended. Bhava arises from heart and silence and not through language – chanting being done by purohit. In reality, Bhava rises from the depth of consciousness. Since we lack awareness of consciousness as the spring of Bhava, we have no understanding of its creation.

The Bhava as it rises from consciousness is so powerful that all our thoughts keep hovering around it. Our intellect looks like a pigmy in comparison to the all- powerful consciousness. For example, as soon as the Bhava for sex arises, our intellect gets paralysed. The reason is that all thoughts at that time veer around sex. Only after the emotions for sex subside, the mind takes over to think of the right and the wrong.

Similarly, the emotion of anger turns us into a monster; attachment makes us blind to the faults of our dear ones and emotion of fear makes us dread our own shadow.

Bhava is also linked to five organs of sense – eyes, ear, nose, mouth and skin. The eye always wants to see beautiful visuals; the ear is keen to hear a soothing sound, the nose is looking for fragrance. In short, Bhava regulates our life as we go through its ups and downs. The sad story is we are unaware of this.

It is through Bhava, that you get a sense of your existence. Again Bhava is involved in giving you a sense of others' existence, you being different from others; making a distinction between your own folks and the rest. Even the feeling of you speaking – all emanate from the area close to your heart. These arise from your conscious mind. Most of us have only that much connection with Chetna (Consciousness); and have no idea of its expanse. There is much more beyond this point in consciousness.

To explain the vastness of Chetna (Consciousness), let's take an example of a man living on the fourth floor of a seven-storey building. He has no idea about the existence of three floors above his flat and three below. He has never opened the doors and windows of his house. Had he done so, he would have at least seen the staircase and got an idea about the existence of one floor up or down. Starting with one floor, he could have possibly climbed up or down and seen all other floors in due course of time.

That man had no curiosity about the world beyond the four walls of his house. He lived within it and died one day and left it for good. After his death, when he was leaving the floor he realised the size of the building. His regret knew no bounds on realising that he was the owner of all other six floors too.

Most of us are like the man in the story. The seven floors denote levels of Chetna (Consciousness). From top to bottom these are:

7. Brahma Chetan Man (Cosmic conscious mind)
6. Samishti Chetan Man (Collective conscious mind)

5. Ati Chetan Man (Superconscious mind)
4. Chetan Man (Conscious mind)
3. Achetan Man (Unconscious mind)
2. Samishti Achetan Man (Collective unconscious mind)
1. Brama Achetan Man (Cosmic unconscious mind)

All our life, we believe that only the conscious mind is consciousness; we remain ignorant of its other levels. The conscious mind is linked to Anahat Chakra (Heart Chakra). The layer just below it is the unconscious mind. It is linked to Manipoorak Chakra (Solar Plexus Chakra). A level deeper lay collective unconscious mind and it is linked to Swadhishthan Chakra (Sacral Chakra). The deepest level of consciousness is the Cosmic unconscious mind, which is linked to Mooladhar Chakra (Root Chakra).

Right above the Anahat Chakra where the conscious mind is located are three upper layers of consciousness. The first layer is the Superconscious mind and it is linked to Vishudha Chakra (Throat Chakra). The layer above is the collective conscious mind and it is linked to Aagya Chakra (Third eyes Chakra). This is also called the sixth sense. The last and top layer is the Cosmic conscious mind and it is connected to Sahasrara Chakra (Crown Chakra).

These subtle layers of consciousness store all information and possibilities right from the creation of the Universe to the infinity and it is possible to decode them. Great personalities like Gautama Buddha have done it. When we are awake, our mind fluctuates between conscious and unconscious levels. While we are asleep, sometimes Chetna delves into layers of consciousness creating interesting dreams for us to see. When the mind is in a state of emptiness, Chetna also travels across these layers.

In this process, many times we come across amazing situations that defy explanation and reasoning. For example, you are thinking of a person and he calls you up. You are bound to start your conversation like this: "What a coincidence; I was just thinking of you!"

His reply, "Even I felt like calling you, as it has been a long time".

We take it as a coincidence and that's not right. The reality is that two persons thought of each other simultaneously because of their collective unconscious mind. In this state, two minds come together. We have no way to make it happen; it happens suddenly.

To explain this phenomenon let's think of a tribesman who has never seen a television set. You leave one along with its remote at his place. He has no idea of this gadget. Suddenly somehow, he switches it on with the remote and sees humans like him inside. Can you imagine his reaction? This is precisely how 'coincidences' happen in our life.

People who know telepathy are able to communicate with persons sitting thousands of miles away. They are conversant with different levels of consciousness and through rigorous practice have come to know the process of connecting with people in far offs places. The influencing of others' minds is also done through the collective unconscious mind.

To understand this at the practical level you should visit a place of worship when devotees are not around. Just sit quietly and feel the vibes. Next, you can visit a bar during non-business hours for a similar experience.

Here, the vibes are quite different. In both places, a different set of people spend a long time together. In a place of worship, people have common Bhava and they generate a large amount of energy of a particular kind.

At the other place, the Bhava of the regular visitors is different and likewise, a different kind of energy is released. For this reason, the vibes at these places are different. When people of the same mindset gather at one place, it emanates special vibes. Their collective unconscious mind plays a role in this.

Like the collective unconscious mind, there is a collective conscious mind also. The wires of our minds are spread out and interlinked like the waves of the Internet. However, most of us fail to realise it due to the lack of a higher level of awareness. This realisation can come only in a higher state of Dhyana.

Our unconscious mind holds a lot of information that we do not always require; it furnishes these as and when we need these urgently. Sometimes, we are unable to recall events from memory yet these are never erased.

These memories are stored in deeper layers of the unconscious mind. Hatha yoga has some exercises that can retrieve the oldest of our memories. We can experience them and afterwards these get stored in their subtle form in our unconsciousness. Sometimes, these memories may come into our conscious mind directly or in a dream yet they always have an impact on our lives indirectly.

This is called the sacrament of consciousness. Older the memories, deeper are these located. The lowest level is called Brahma Achetan Man or Cosmic Unconscious Mind. It has secrets of the creation of the universe and memories from all our previous births.

The upper levels of consciousness have all the information about the future. Invoking these makes one go through supernatural experiences. When it reaches the collective conscious mind that person would know everything about others and can foresee the future. He is bestowed with powers of clairvoyance. If someone reaches Brahma Chetan Man (Cosmic conscious mind), he becomes a Bhagwan in the human body, like Gautam Buddha, Mahavir, Guru Nanak Dev and many others in terms of knowledge about the ultimate truth.

By doing intense Sadhna (spiritual practice) of seven Chakras, one can travel across layers of consciousness. However, it is not an easy task; one has to practice rigorously through Dhyana based on breathing exercises.

God is also called Param Chaitanya, Pure or Cosmic consciousnesses. Trees, plants, insects, animals and humans all have common consciousnesses. The difference lies in the quantity and quality. Plants have traces of consciousness and yet need vital energy in equal measures. Plants have feelings, though at a low level. A plant changes its feelings for a gardener after he ruthlessly prunes them while they respond positively to one who nurtures them. The plants can tell a friend from an adversary. However, plants do not have the level of consciousness that can build their mind. However, plants also generate vibes and we are linked to them through collective consciousness and collective unconsciousness. We have different feelings about seeing a dead flower lying on the ground and a blossom.

Insects have a higher level of consciousness than plants and birds. The mammals have a higher degree of consciousness and for this reason, some animals like dogs and cats follow human commands after being trained. Especially dogs, they even understand human emotions. There are instances of dogs, cows and other animals giving up food after the death of their master. They can understand human emotions and catch the vibes well while insects cannot. It is due to a large gap between the growth of consciousness of insects and humans. The gap is less in the case of animals.

The growth of human being happens at the level of body and consciousness. According to Charles Darwin, humans have evolved from animals. During this process, they have passed through many cycles of death and rebirth. Alongside the bodily evolution from animal to human, the consciousness of humans also evolved.

Indian Philosophy says that an organism goes through 84 hundred thousand (84 lakh) rebirths before being born as a human. This is the precise story of his bodily evolution and that of his consciousness. Today human consciousness is the most evolved and the reason why humans are a superior life form.

Nature has given human consciousness a vast bandwidth from Cosmic Unconsciousness to Cosmic Consciousnesses. It is up to humans to explore the spectrum of their vast consciousness and that is the purpose of human life.

Have you ever thought why sometimes a human being behaves in a beastly manner while he looks like a divine incarnation through his behaviour the other time? How can the same human being have contrasting traits? It is because his experiences of a past life as a beast are embedded in the layers of his Consciousnesses as is his yearning to merge with divinity. The beauty of consciousness is that the deeper you go to explore it, the higher you rise. This process of search is Adhyatma.

RECAP

- The feeling of your being comes from an area around the heart in your body. However, we, the humans, remain unaware of the fact that above and below the spot from where this particular feeling emanates lay a more active zone.
- Our consciousness has seven levels. However, most of us spend our lives with a conscious mind without delving into or thinking about the other levels.

- Below the conscious mind lay another layer called the unconscious mind. Below the unconscious mind is the layer called the collective unconscious mind. The lowermost level is the cosmic unconscious mind.

- There are three layers of consciousness above the conscious mind. The first layer that is close to the conscious mind is Ati Chetan Man or superconscious mind. Another layer above the superconscious mind is called the collective conscious mind. It is also known as the sixth sense of the Third Eye. The topmost layer is Brahma Chetan or Cosmic conscious mind.

- Nothing ever gets erased from our unconscious mind. It has memories about the past right from the creation of the Universe to one's past births. The conscious mind layers have all the information about the future.

- When consciousness reaches the superconscious mind, the person has a supernatural vision. When it reaches the collective conscious mind, the person knows everything about others and can have premonitions about future events.

❑❑❑

12

CHAPTER

The Wandering Mind

Why do we succeed in one task and fail in another? Any task undertaken in a state of consciousness is bound to succeed while the one done without it would lead us to failure or unsatisfactory results. In the mundane world, tasks get accomplished even when done in a state of unconsciousness. However, such an approach does not work in the realm of spirituality. You may end up wasting your time in case you start your spiritual journey without being in a state of consciousness.

Here the question arises how could one do a task while in unconsciousness? The short and simple answer is that being conscious is not simply as we are. It has a connotation which is different from what most of us understand.

Human beings live in three stages: awake, asleep and dreaminess. In sleep, we are unaware of everything; in dreaminess, we see things that turn out to be false at the end. In both these conditions, we are unconscious. The tricky condition is when we are awake. In this stage, we do all our 'karma' (actions) and yet mostly our mind is not present at the same place where the body is.

Let's take the case of your routine morning drive to the office. Mostly your body is driving while the mind has already reached the office and you are contemplating your moves for the day. Physically your mind is on the road and yet your mind is in office. All of a sudden, you see a speeding truck coming in your direction. In a microsecond, your heart feels a thud; in a jerky movement your mind comes alive to the situation and you realise you have survived a close shave with death.

Now you are fully conscious and aware. The mind can again go wandering; there is no surety that the consciousness will linger on. You thank God for saving you and curse yourself for driving so unmindfully. Now, your mind has reached your home thinking of your family. You are visualizing the plight of your family in case you had got injured or died in the accident. Next, you think of buying gifts for your children on return from the office. You have decided on the gifts and also visualize the shop from where you will buy these.

After a narrow escape from death, logically your mind should be focused on work in the office. After all, it was your thoughts of the office that landed you in a dangerous situation. The mind has wandered, again.

The mind is a wanderer. It leaves you as a body at a place and moves on to other spaces. We are unable to concentrate on things the thoughts of that were trigged by the very mind. For example, your mind feels like eating a particular food. You buy its ingredients from the market and cook it only to find your mind has lost interest. Logically, the mind should be present to taste the food that it wanted so badly and for which it made you slog. However, when you taste it, the mind has moved on, probably to the experience of tasting the dish last time. It is comparing the two situations. Even while thinking of a dish it made you cook, it is not present in the moment.

The mind never lets you be peaceful and it is a reason why you are unable to do a task with full consciousness. Ironically, if the job is done well in the end, it is the mind that is happy and satisfied. At times, the mind dissuades you from pursuing a task and you too go with it. You stop bothering and take a casual attitude towards life. The mind plays games because it has a subtle fear of losing control.

Since we do not understand it, we get used to being misled by the mind. The only way to change this habit is to do Dhyana.

Is Mind's Wandering Bad?

While attempting Dhyana, we do face a challenge in keeping our mind stable and focused because of the mind's innate nature. Humans are often told that a wandering mind is not good for them. Is this common belief about the mind right? Those who talk about it have also heard it from others and there is no tangible proof of the wandering mind being a bad thing. Are we the victim of the Chinese whispers on the nature of the mind? It seems this idea has come to us as a distorted version of the original one. The fact is that the wandering of the mind is a sign of life. To get rid of this habit of the mind, we should get rooted and firmed up. There are many ways to make the mind static and firm up. Likewise, there are many ways to slow down the speed of the mind; the repeated chanting of any word – often mistaken as a mantra – is one such way.

However, a question arises: is weakening the mind and slowing its pace worth it? Do we gain from it? The mind stops wandering when we are asleep, in a state of unconsciousness or under the influence of drugs or alcohol. Perhaps, this is the reason why some sadhus smoke weed. Is it an achievement? What does one gain from making the mind weak and slow?

Slowing down the mind does not help us achieve anything. On the contrary, it weakens both our intellect and willpower. It is safe to say that it limits the dynamics of our intellect, making it static and that's not quite helpful.

It may appear that I am approving the wandering nature of the mind. Actually, I am making an argument against its slowing down. A racing mind is not bad for us. The question is about the quality of the mind's speed. The speed can be that of a madman and that is not desirable. The directionless speed will do us no good; the speed should be with a purpose and directed at a target. In that case, speed is very useful.

To explain it, we take the example of a steady stream and a stray cloud that has drifted from a larger one. The stream is moving at a certain pace towards its merger with the sea. On the other hand, the stray cloud has lost its original path due to its habit of wandering and will never reach the ocean. The flow and speed of the river are good; that of the directionless and wandering cloud is not. This brings us to the point that the speed and movement of the mind are not bad; only if the speed is directionless, it is not good. This is the real meaning of the need to rein in a wandering mind as mentioned in ancient texts.

To understand the difference between the regular and the deranged ways of the mind, let's go to your experience of reading this text. If you were not consistent in reading this text and had jumped from a few sentences to some paragraph in no particular order, you would have failed to reach this point in pursuing your desire to understand the mind. So the flow and speed in itself are not harmful but if it gets deranged it is.

We manage our mind in two ways: one is to let it drift like a lunatic; the other is to slow its speed by chanting some mantras repeatedly. We have no idea of the third way: Dhyana. Yes, in fact, in Dhyana, the speed of the mind is required. We should use the speed of the mind to reach our target. There is no gain in manipulating its speed and making it lose its energy. One would wonder how to prepare such a mind?

Had Gautam Buddha become happy and contented with his power as a King and his riches, he would have never achieved Nirvana. The discontentment of the mind with mundane things like money, palaces, comfort etc. is a key factor in taking us on a revolutionary path of the ultimate truth.

Once, an emperor went to meet a mystic in his hut. The Mystic was not there; he was working in the garden, close by. His wife asked the emperor to take a seat while she would call her husband from the garden. The emperor didn't sit and said he would wait outside. The lady spread a mat for him and yet he kept pacing to and fro. The lady told her husband about the visitor. She told him that the emperor behaved like a madman as he didn't sit despite her cajoling.

The mystic replied, "He is not mad. I have seen him sitting most of the time. He is the King; he will not sit just anywhere. There is no suitable place in our house for him, that's why he didn't sit on the mat".

The Monarch in the story personifies the mind that never stays in one place lest it becomes content. We will never have a throne that can be inviting for the mind to stay put and make it give up its nature of wandering.

However, as we watch a good movie or sit by the seaside or a mountain, the mind seldom wanders. For some time, we get fully absorbed in the scene and feel relaxed. It gives a different kind of peace in which the mind does not play its usual games. We essentially enjoy being absorbed in some situations and the mind recuperates. You will notice that you experience happiness only when you get absorbed in something like reading an interesting book or pursuing a hobby. When the mind is resting it creates happiness though in the physical world it can never rest for long.

The mind rests only in the divine power, called Parmatma (God). That position is ideal for it to sit in silence and yet exude authority. It is a divine blessing that your mind does not get stuck at just anything. If it was not so maybe your mind would take fancy of a heap of trash and get stuck there.

The day your mind becomes peaceful you will realise its wandering nature has made you closer to the divine. This peace is fluid and makes us alive. The mind will take you everywhere and yet not settle at any place until it gets closer to the Divinity. The day your live mind becomes peaceful, you must sense that you have reached closer to Parmatma (Divinity).

Does it mean that as soon as your mind is at peace, you have reached the Divine? It is the other way round – the day you will get even a glimpse of divinity, your mind automatically gets stable. However, this stability does not make the mind static; it makes it lively and more aware. But most of us try to achieve this in the opposite and wrong way – We try to stop the thoughts and that makes the mind fixated like the roots of a big tree. This process will not help.

Reboot Yourself

The methods we practice to make the mind peaceful are often flawed. These mostly end up in benumbing the mind and it getting fixated. Unfortunately, in all our ignorance, we call it Dhyana. However, the fact is that for Dhyana, we do not have to strain for getting into it. Let this be clear that for Dhyana, one does not require any practice. You simply have to do nothing and it cannot be easier than that.

However, the simple task of not doing anything is the most challenging for us. Just close your eyes for five minutes and sit with a resolve that you will not do any action. This could turn out to be the most difficult part of your day; you will feel like scratching your skin and hundreds of thoughts will emerge in the mind. This is because all our life we have practised thinking of something and getting rid of this habit for even five minutes is diffcult. For Dhyana, we have to unlearn everything; just sit at a quiet place with our eyes closed. Dhyana happens when the mind is resting. So, the mind cannot rest in the middle of some practice. Practice and complete rest cannot go together.

Given its mercurial mature, even the idea of unlearning will trigger a multitude of thoughts in the mind. What we need to do is akin to rebooting a computer or any electronic gadget in silence, with strict instruction not to press any key or click the mouse till it is over. The flow of thoughts makes the mind go into usual overdrive.

Controlling the mind does not need any practice; it happens when we live with awareness. We should remain aware of the thoughts flowing in our mind, do even the smallest task with full awareness and act as a mute spectator to the thoughts emanating in the mind without getting involved. Never try to stop the flow.

While being a spectator to the ideas of mind, your effort should be to do your work with total awareness and keep a tab on whether the thoughts being generated by the mind are relevant to the task you are involved in. If your thoughts are about things other than what you are into, then you are not in total awareness.

If you follow this method, you will see the mind has shifted the goalpost in your favour. Since you didn't interfere or try to cease the mind, it has become peaceful. This process has to be practised since it will help you remain aware of the Nadi and the Tatva also. You will realise the tasks done with full awareness get you the best results.

RECAP

- We live in three stages: awake, asleep and dreaming. While asleep, we are unconscious; in the dreamy stage, we live in an illusion.

- It is only in the state of awakening that we do all our 'karma'. However, during this stage too, our mind is away from what our body is engaged in. Even while we are awake, we are not fully conscious.

- From ancient time, humans are told that the mind is restless and this restlessness is not good. Is it a case of Chinese whispers; the restlessness of mind may not be bad and it is a case of highly distorted reality that is coming to us.

- The mind is always exploring new horizons; it gets easily bored and, in the process, goads us to achieve more. Like a rich man is never satisfied with the money and riches he has acquired; he is always yearning for more.

- The restlessness of the mind is a great blessing. Had it not been so, we would be contented with the mundane and ordinary. This quality of mind takes us on the path of spirituality. If the riches and luxury of a palace have been enough to make Buddha's mind contented, he would have never renounced everything and treaded on a revolutionary path.

- In order to make the mind stable, it needs to unlearn everything; in a way, this process is comparable to the rebooting of electronic systems like mobile or a computer.

- The mind wanders till it reaches divinity.

❑❑❑

13

CHAPTER

Dhyana Just Happens

Imagine a situation when you are eagerly waiting for someone. Your mind is focused on the sounds coming from outside; you do not want to miss even the faintest of these. Also, you are able to tell one sound from the other and suddenly, it seems, your ability to pick and understand sounds has increased manifold. Finally, you get to hear the familiar sound of the footsteps you had been eagerly awaiting. This precision on sounds comes as you are in awareness and your mind focused. If your mind was not focused, you would have never noticed any sound outside of the room.

Sometimes, it happens that we are not able to hear sounds that others do. Only after you are asked to listen to it carefully, you do follow the sound. This is what we commonly call paying attention. We all have the power of being aware yet we can use it by making an effort.

However, in spiritual parlance, 'Dhyana' is not like paying attention or focus; it has a different connotation. This chapter will also deal with the most prevalent confusion and a mix-up between Dhyana and meditation.

Meditation and Dhyana

The English word 'meditation' has a different meaning in different cultures. Meditation is defined as a practice where an individual uses a technique – such as mindfulness, or focus of the mind on a particular object, thought, or activity–to train attention and awareness, and achieve a mentally clear and emotionally calm and stable state.

Dictionaries give both the original Latin meaning of "thinking deeply about (something)"; as well as the popular usage of "focusing one's mind for a period of time", "the act of giving your attention to only one thing, either as a religious activity or as a way of becoming calm and relaxed", and "to engage in mental exercise (such as concentrating on one's breathing or repetition of a mantra) for the purpose of reaching a heightened level of spiritual awareness".

All techniques used in meditation are aimed at making the mind learn to focus on something–a picture of God, a religious man, an idol or even a mantra or other sound.

At times, our wandering mind is exhausted and in case it can focus, the brain relaxes and conserves its energy.

Interestingly, it is again the mind at work when it is trying to focus. This means that while normally thoughts keep flooding the mind always, in meditation, it is preoccupied with only one thought. This means that the mind is still active, though in a limited sense in meditation. Dhyana is different.

The mind has three stages. By now, we have realised the two stages of mind: wandering stage and focused stage. In its third stage, the mind is devoid of thoughts; it is blank. This stage is called Dhyana. In this, the mind is no player.

In Dhyana, we alienate our consciousness from the world and allow it to rest. In spiritual terms, Dhyana is a process that leads us to realise our inner power that makes us aware of the world around us. Our sense of consciousness makes us aware of the things on which we focus our attention. So, when have to discover the source of consciousness, it is imperative that we focus on it.

Dhyana is the only action that happens without any input. Yes, we simply do not have to do anything about it. We are required to block all our usual actions that have become our second nature. In Dhyana, we reach the centre of awareness where lies pure consciousness. You must know that our sense of awareness is a tiny speck of pure consciousness. On this scale, it is beyond our imagination to think of the expanses and the power of pure consciousness.

Going into Dhyana is easy; it can happen in a second and we are not required to do anything for it. What can be easier than doing nothing? However, this seemingly easier task turns out to be a big challenge. Our mind is accustomed to focusing on many things simultaneously and that becomes difficult to give up. It wastes energy in focusing on useless thoughts and when it is required to conserve them, the mind gets nervous.

Suppose you are sitting idle and are lost in thoughts and someone asks you, "Where are you lost?"

"Nothing, I was just thinking?"

If he insists on a detailed reply, you may not be able to explain. Of what use is thinking if you can't figure it out? Yet this is the reality of our mind. We become addicted to thinking and never practice doing nothing. This makes the task of doing nothing difficult.

I asked a friend, who practised meditation for years, how does he do it. He said he kept his mind focused on a chant. Is the focus on a chant, not meditation? My question made him pensive. He asked me the method of doing it. I told him to close his eyes for five minutes and sit quietly. No need to focus; let the mind have no work.

He tried it and five minutes was too long a period for his mind to not do anything. Within three minutes he opened his eyes and said, “It is very diffcult. How can anyone sit like that? It’s just not possible for me...!” He admitted he could not do without keeping his mind focused on something. Keeping his mind thought-free was difficult.

Meditation is useful but Dhyana is different. Dhyana happens in the depths of consciousness and beyond it at the level of pure consciousness. In it, the mind ceases to exist; it survives a deep slumber. In the stage of dreaminess, the mind can cease to exist but in that situation, we do not know how to make use of it as we are not aware while asleep. However, in Dhyana we are aware and that is why we can connect with our inner-self. Meditation is an English word. There is no word for Dhyana in this language.

There are seven processes linked with “Hat Yoga” and of these Dhyana is the seventh one. One must understand all of these to realise the meaning of Dhyana. Attempting meditation without understanding these will be akin to someone trying to jump to the seventh step of a staircase in one go bypassing six steps and without knowing about the existence of the 8th step. These are:

1. Yama (external discipline)
2. Niyam (internal discipline)
3. Asana (sitting posture)
4. Pranayama (breath control)

5. Pratyahara (withdrawal of senses)
6. Dharna (concentration)
7. Dhyana (meditative absorption)
8. Samadhi (union, integration)

Nowadays, it has become fashionable for people to join meditation sessions in large air-conditioned halls under the aegis of a Yogi or Guru. If the participants are found gossiping after attending the session, it is sure a waste of time. Instead, one could have spent time with a friend, played a sport or a game or even watched a movie.

Some people meditate in the belief that it would transform them and they end up in disappointment. Such an exercise is a waste of time and energy and therefore suffocating.

Each human being is born with an innate nature, called 'Svabhava' (Hindi). It is composed of 'Sva' meaning self and 'Bhava' meaning Nature. Each human has a different sense of being and it is exclusive. Is it possible to change yourself by a few minutes of meditation? The very exercise claiming to transform you into someone else is torturous. Or maybe you are a victim of a trend or have fallen for the fancy advertisement of the teaching shops that claim to change your life through meditation.

My idea is not to dissuade you from meditation. I am trying to differentiate between real meditation and its touted versions. The purpose of Dhyana is self- realisation. It is not about getting into the self but seeing the reality of the self. The eyes are meant for humans to see the world outside and not inside. We need the 'real' eye or the Third Eye for self-realisation. This happens through Dhyana.

Dhyana is a state of mind that cannot be achieved; it just happens to a person. To understand it, let's take an example from our daily life. Can you become angry with someone's directions? Can you love, hate and take pity on someone because you are asked to? We can act to show these emotions but not by design. These emotions come up at an appropriate time effortlessly. Dhyana also happens like this: without an effort or scheming. We can, however, create congenial conditions for Dhyana.

If consciousness were a circle, its centre is our real self. Our mind keeps revolving around the centre not realising the real place. Atma or the soul is the centre of our existence but since the mind is fed by the five senses it has the tendency to look out. The mind is predisposed towards experiencing the outer world and, therefore, does not go to the centre of the consciousness. It makes us experience the outer world at large. However, when we are feeling extreme joy and ecstasy the mind comes to that centre momentarily and quickly returns to the mundane world. When we discover the centre through Dhyana, we experience bliss and the state of staying there is called Samadhi.

We know that the mind is the creator of thoughts and if thoughts are deleted the mind ceases to exist. Similarly, after occasionally touching the centre of consciousness, it leaves quickly. Only a blank mind merges into Atma (Soul), leading to self-realisation. The eye is just an instrument to see the world. The question arises: Who is seeing? The dazzle of the outer world never lets us think about this.

The real you is the entity that experiences what organs of sense convey. This realisation dawns on us only after our disconnection with the outer world. Till that time, we believe that the outer world is the real one–conveyed by the mind. Since the mind always moves in the space of radius, we never think of the centre. Our real self lies in the centre and it is called Atma or pure consciousness. This process of reaching there is regulated by the subtle reactions of the breath.

How Dhyana Happens?

On earth, we naturally balance our body. A toddler has to learn to balance before he is able to walk. However, the same habit of balancing becomes a hindrance while learning to swim. For this, we have to unlearn this tendency of balancing to be able to learn swimming. This involves giving up control over the body and leaving it limp. Try this out in the water and you will drown. Likewise, we have to discard all we have learnt so far for getting into Dhyana.

Learning to do nothing is the hardest. We somehow manage to calm our conscious mind while we sit for Dhyana. However, the unconscious mind keeps sending us memories, thoughts and visions. Since the unconscious mind is aware of our task of Dhyana, it would send us related pictures, thoughts and images. In this stage, some would feel as if they are flying; others may have experience of passing through a dark tunnel or crossing a river of fire. This is certainly not Dhyana!

Dhyana is a stage in which our mind goes blank and it is filled with emptiness; no wave-like thought rises from its placid sea. The surface of this lake is like a mirror that reflects something that cannot be portrayed in words. Eyes cannot see it nor can we experience it.

This is the beginning of the journey to our real self. One gets in Dhyana when all our five senses, body actions and functions stop and only pure consciousness prevails. It starts with one learning to sit in a posture comfortably at a stretch for at least a couple of hours. This state of the mind is called Asana. Often as soon as you sit for Dhyana you feel like scratching your skin and moving your feet. The first move is to make the body used to sit quietly – this practice is called Sadhna. This process rids you of your thoughts.

To understand the mind from the perspective of Dhyana, let's assume you are standing at point A. You can see the road ahead but not the one behind you. You move and cover a lot of distance only to realise that your destination point B is located on the road behind point A. Now you have to go in the reverse direction to reach point A and restart your journey to point B.

The same is the case with us. The mind has taken us away from our real self. The destination of our journey is the centre of consciousness and our mind is not even in its radius; it wades through in the outer world. The first task is to bring the mind back into the radius of the circle of consciousness. From there begins the inner journey to the centre of the consciousness and the emptiness of the mind. Interestingly, thoughts deflect us from the centre of consciousness into the radius and the outside.

However, we can make use of the same thoughts to undertake the inner journey to our core though in a different way.

Find the Gap

We must understand the role played by the mind in propelling us to move to the wrong destination. On realising our mistake we first return to the starting point and begin a new journey to the real destination.

Interestingly, returning the mind does not allow us to use the same thoughts that had made us undertake the first journey. Here, we have to behave like a disinterested bystander to the flowing thoughts.

Thoughts flow one after another. However, if you pay attention, you will find a subtle gap between the two thoughts. As soon as the gap is located, we can break the sequence of thoughts and use them to get into the mind. Though this can be done anytime, an early morning gives faster results. It can also be done before going to bed at least two hours after having the meal.

For this exercise, you should choose a quiet place. If that's not possible, just use your mobile phone earplugs. The place should have dim light. Use a yoga mat, a woollen rug or a blanket to sit on. Make sure your body does not touch bare surfaces like floor and wall. You can also sit in a chair or anywhere except on spring mattresses since the spine cannot balance it on that. You have to sit for at least 40 minutes continuously.

Keep your spine straight; slightly bend your neck and slowly close your eyes. Inhale slowly for five minutes making your stomach rise like a balloon and exhale, slowly. While exhaling, your stomach should flatten. In case you know how to check the Nadi, find out which one is active.

Stay calm and just see what thoughts are passing in your mind. Do not get involved in these thoughts; watch them like a bystander. You should neither try to tweak the thought nor try to block it. Let it flow and you remain aware. In case we have an experience in between feel it consciously; do not get carried away.

Recall your experience of crossing a road. You would look at the car coming on the road and pass by. You just observed it and didn't move along. Next, you shifted your focus to the second car. The thoughts are also like cars on the road. They come one after another in a pattern.

You just have to observe them. Likewise, you let the thoughts in your mind pass one after another. After some practice, you will realise there is a small gap between two consecutive thoughts. It can be easily done with our conscious mind. After some practice, you will realise your thoughts are dwindling. Actually, the unconscious mind that sends these thoughts is not used to be monitored. It will slow down. At this stage, you can find the gap of the length of which varies from very short to the long.

This is exactly like crossing the road. We can cross when the gap between the two vehicles is long. Likewise, we can use the gap of thoughts to reach from one level of mind to another. During this phase, remain aware of your breathing and notice the changes. You will realise breathing is slowing down gradually. Again, keep an eye on the breathing like a spectator or witness. This is the beginning of the journey of the soul.

After some time, when the flow of thoughts in your conscious mind considerably slows down, you will be a bystander.

This exercise will gradually make you experience various levels of the mind. Again, you do not have to get involved; just enjoy the experiences. Continuous practice and awareness are the keys to success. You cannot describe your experiences in words. You can begin with a 40-minute schedule and stretch it further to any period.

Why 40-Minute Schedule?

Why is the regimen of 40-minute essential? Some would argue that we should begin with a 15-20-minute schedule and increase it gradually. Is it possible to boil water in phases? The first day boil it to 30 degrees; the next day by another 30; then by 40 – can we make water reach boiling point in a staggered manner?

In the 40-minute exercise, there are more chances of reading the Tatva flowing in the breath. This time frame is also required for Sushumna to run its course. Since it is during Sushumna's active phase that Aakash Tatva flows in the breath and that is best-suited for Dhyana and meditation.

For this, one does not need the guidance of a Guru as your real Guru is sitting inside you. A Guru can put you on the track to a destination and can give you tips on how to correct course in case you digress. The journey of consciousness has to be traversed alone; it is a personal experience. Consider it like the experience of a deep-sea diver. He can shoot a video for you to see underwater life. However, he would never be able to convey his underwater experience in words.

Most young people may wonder why should one opt for Dhyana; Isn't life beautiful otherwise too? Others believe that Dhyana connects you to God and they may not be in hurry to do so. Others may feel they are tied up with their lives and cannot even think of Dhyana. They need to know that Dhyana would help them accomplish their routine tasks in a better way.

It is true that one cannot reach the divine (God) without Dhyana and that is the ultimate goal for all humans. In between, there are a plethora of targets to be achieved. One hour of Dhyana can generate the energy required by a human body to do all his routine tasks for the day.

In a gymnasium, we first work on our muscles so that the tissues break. Thereafter, this exercise is stopped to give rest to muscles. We eat protein that helps repair and build tissues. This is the regime of bodybuilding. Can we do all this without taking a proper sleep?

If we do not sleep for four days, the body will not be able to stand up. Exercise and proteins can build the body but the energy required to run it is generated during sleep. Through sleep, in the night we recharge our batteries to get enough energy for the next day. We get the same amount of energy from sleeping for eight hours and doing meditation/dhyana for one hour.

Therefore, one hour of meditation is enough to keep you energized throughout the day.

During the day our senses imbibe a lot of unwanted scenes, sounds and images for our unconscious mind. These memories are like unwanted cookies that slow down our mobile phones and computers.

The process of focusing on the breath or a thought deletes a lot of unwanted memories, sharpens our intellect and increases the power of concentration. Like bodybuilding exercise, we also need to exercise for the health and growth of our mind and intellect. Unlike bodybuilding, this exercise has no side effects.

Our eternal pursuit of happiness is meant to take us to the source of happiness. Man does not know that the fountainhead of happiness lies within him. Our real self is nothing but happiness and ecstasy. It is called Sachchidananda meaning Satya, the truth, Chita (Pure mind) and Anand (ecstasy).

Ecstasy is the other name of the truth about the mind and the man is constantly in its search. It lay within us while we keep looking for it everywhere. We are born out of ecstasy as our parents created us in it. Therefore, our real self is pure ecstasy and seeing it is called 'Darshan'.

Ignorance is like darkness while knowledge is light. In reality, darkness does not exist; it is the absence of light. However, within ourselves, we are not able to experience anything without light. It vanishes as soon as the light falls. Is it possible for the darkness to overpower the light? Not really.

Like darkness, ignorance is not an entity. It is a lack of knowledge. The ignorance about a subject lasts only till we acquire knowledge about it. Light and knowledge are the only constants. The vividness of outside life is actually darkness in front of the lamp of light that lay within us. We carry an impression of the world through our five senses. These senses get acclimatized to only carrying a signal from the outside while in reality, they are capable of seeing both inside and outside worlds. The dreams we see in sleep, the sound of cramps in the stomach, the images we see with closed eyes are all proof of their two-way capacity. The senses are oblivious of the inner-self because they have never practised following the inside happenings. The epicentre of the world around us lies inside. Dhyana leads us to this point.

There is no difference between the world inside and outside of the body. The outside world is also a reflection of the Divine. It is like we see a reflection of the moon in a lake and believe it to be the real Moon. While we go inside the lake to grab it, we end up losing even the reflection of it. Likewise, when we run after material successes, our happiness spreads out and vanishes like the reflection of the moon in the lake. What we see in the world is a reflection of the Divine and not Divinity.

For this reason, the world is called Maya, an illusion. Maya is composed of two Sanskrit words 'Ma' meaning the visible and 'Yaa' meaning that is not. The dazzling world outside is a reflection of the world inside us. A reflection is always the opposite of the object. In order to get the reality of the object, one has to move in the opposite direction of the reflection. However, we, humans do it the wrong way. We tend to run in the opposite direction of the real object – towards the reflection. That is why we are always chasing happiness while it lay inside us.

The Upanishads and other ancient texts tell us that the inside and outside worlds are not two. Interestingly, these do not say that the two worlds are one. The reflection is an entity the existence of which cannot be denied. Hence the texts have used a measured expression.

The pure consciousness, Atma or soul, is not different from the divine (God). The soul is part of divinity and it means ‘I’ and God are not separate entities. Self-realisation is therefore seeing the Divine. It should be clear that this self-realisation is not about knowing yourself through the ‘gate to self’. It is about knowing our true self through the real eyes, the sixth sense.

You cannot see yourself through your eyes. You cannot see even your face with eyes. We can only see the reflection of our face in the mirror. In this, the right side of the face is on the left and left on the right. The sixth sense or the real eye opens at the behest of Aagya Chakra. It is only after reaching this Chakra that we can move ahead in our journey of self-realisation.

For achieving self-realisation, one has to clean his mind. This cleansing can happen only through Dhyana. The rest of the process just happens; it is the handiwork of the Divinity. As a body, we are the children of our parents; as a soul, we belong to the Supreme Power or God. He alone can give his real love and happiness. Love, as we know is selfish and conditional; two people in love have expectations from each other. Some people make sacrifices in love and take it as unconditional love while it is renunciation. In unconditional love, there are no two parties and hence no sacrifice.

True love is what we, as toddlers, receive from our mother and the one from the Almighty. The moment we give up our ego and cleanse our mind, He steps in. Here, ego refers to the feeling that I am a different entity from the Almighty. The reality is we are one. It is a basic rule that our mind does not let us decipher.

A child is a form of Godliness. His mind is pure as he gets happiness from just anything – a pebble, playing in mud or a cheap toy. On the other hand, an adult craves riches and once he gets it he is worried about securing it. The fear overshadows his happiness.

We create mind by building it with our memories. Over the conscious mind lay a layer of intellect and in between the two is a thin layer of awareness. Awareness takes the right decisions for our life. By using awareness, we can imbibe the simplicity, coolness and unselfishness of a child. Being aware will leave the difference between you and a child only at the level of intellect.

In this situation, one's intellect will keep growing but the mind starts deleting useless memories that are behind the urge to chase the illusionary happiness. Life will become simpler and easy. With being aware, you can embark on a fresh journey in the company of consciousness and unlimited intellect. Our intellect is embedded between the layers and hence remains inert mostly. This new journey is about moving from conscious to superconscious mind; then to the collective conscious mind and finally to the cosmic conscious mind. Here the journey ends; there is nothing further to yearn for. At this stage, language becomes irrelevant.

Saints like Kabir had reached this stage of their spiritual journey. That is the reason why an unlettered Kabir wrote highly evocative poetry.

During this journey the mind will not cease to exist; it will not be your master. Its capacity to function independently will stop; it will listen to the intellect. The growth of intellect leads to will power.

One often hears people make excuses for indulging in violence and become angry: "I was calm; his remarks made me lose my cool". The speaker is suggesting that he is remotely controlled. Just imagine what all you will be seen doing with your control in the hands of some person or a force. He can use our senses to make us dance to his tunes. The reaction of blaming others for our reaction is because of the past memories in our unconscious mind.

All the above is real knowledge and it can be acquired by listening to the Guru inside us. If you do that, you will be a sanyasi, (mendicant) in the true sense and not the one identified through his saffron or coloured robes and having memorizing texts. A mendicant is the one who leads a life as per the rules of the Divinity; not by the parameters set by humans. We are not created to bc slaves; the purpose of our life is to achieve bliss by knowing about our real self.

The goal of human life is to meet the Divine. To get there, the man has to forgo his ego that arises from his sense of his existence. That can be done only through Dhyana. Also, it is the only way to dissociate oneself from the feeling of the body, mind, senses; the remaining of our existence is God and that's our real self.

Sant Kabir has summed it up succinctly in this couplet:

"Tera tere paas hai, apne me hi tatol,
rai badhi na til ghata, hari bolo hari bol".

English Translation

"Your God is within you. The search has to be within yourself. What lies within you is not even a wee bit lesser than God nor is it a spec bigger. You must find the God that resides within you".

In the Hindi text, Kabir purposely uses the word 'tatol' and not search. The meaning of 'tatol' is an intense search done by sifting through various things. (It has no English equivalent). Kabir is directing one to go through a painstaking process of sifting through various layers of consciousness to reach Him, for there is no pinpointed place where He resides. By closing our eyes, we get into darkness and can search for things only through sifting. This is Dhyana.

Kabir says that there is not an iota of difference between what resides inside you and others. We need not go to the Himalayas in search of Him; a quiet corner at your house will do.

It is possible that even when we are in the Himalayas, our mind is wandering in the noisy world that we have come physically far from. Someone can acquire a state of peacefulness while being part of a crowd. It depends on how much our senses can overwhelm our mind. Kabir asks us to descend into our inside for Hari, the Lord who takes away all our pain.

RECAP

- There are many techniques of meditation however Dhyana is different from meditation. Due to the limitation of the English language, we have no equivalents to translate terms like Japa, Yama, Niyam, Dhaarna, Pranayama and Samadhi – steps that are required to be taken before one can do Dhyana.
- Without understanding these, even attempting Dhyana (meditation) will be like someone trying to jump onto the seventh step of a staircase in one go.
- While swimming, one has to unlearn the way he balances the body; it requires unlearning.
- The moment one leaves control of the body in water, swimming comes naturally. Likewise, one has to unlearn everything to get into Dhyana.

- Through Drishta Bhava one can learn to keep oneself away from the thoughts and memories of the mind.
- Dhyana happens in a state of emptiness. It is called the zero state of mind.
- The opposite of reflection is the object. The outside world is a reflection of the Divine that resides within us.

❑❑❑

14

CHAPTER

Chakra Sadhna

By now readers are familiar with three Nadis – Ida, Pingla and Sushumna and the Chakras formed at their intersections. I am often shocked to see the casual claims on invoking Chakras made in the schools that have sprung all over the world. The internet has a mine of unverified claims about Chakras. Some of these shops seem to treat the art of 'Chakra alignment' the same way as the wheels of an automobile. Their idea of Chakra as a wheel is based on the literal translation of the Sanskrit word. The commercialization of Chakras saddens me because Chakra Sadhna is a high level of practice. It cannot be done with the 'wheels' getting 'aligned' in the garages called Chakra alignment workshops!

The human body is like a vast city with ten gates. In the Indian school of spiritualism and philosophy, these gates are the body's inlets. Nine of these are the mouth, a pair of nostrils, eyes and ears; reproductive system and rectal outlets. The most important, the tenth one is located in the top portion of the head and is called Brahmarandra. It is also known as Crown Chakra (Sahasrara). It is the exact spot that is the soft part of the new-born's skull.

Humans are born with no bone at this spot and it firms up as a bone grows gradually. This is considered the tenth gate of the body.

The spiritual journey is all about the search for this tenth gate. The purpose of the Chakra Sadhna is this discovery. This Sadhna is done with one's vision inwards and energy released out of the body. A person who is able to open this gate is like a stream that flows smoothly towards its inevitable merger with the sea and becomes the sea. In essence, the opening of this door leads one to merge his self with the divinity. This is the ultimate target of a yogi. It is also called Moksha.

The Sadhna of Seven Chakras is the process of carrying energy from the lowest Chakra to Brahmarandra or Crown Chakra. I am based at those who claim that it can be done within a few days. They charge a hefty fee from gullible clients.

In today's globalised world, humans have become copycats and they are in a rat race. We are trying to be like the rich man we know, the most stylish person we met the other day or the physically powerful neighbour etc. Humans have thus developed a flock mentality.

Following others in fashion and style is fine but it is not beneficial for Chakra Sadhna.

Chakra Sadhna is a high level of Sadhna and should be attempted in all seriousness. In tune with the book's attempt to simplify the complex thoughts for readers, a simple method of Chakra Sadhna will be presented here. However, anyone serious about this should first meet a Yoga Guru and learn the nuances of Pranayama. You must learn about practices like Rechak, Purak and Kumbhaka. Also, one should practise Dhyana. Sadhna should be done either before or after dhyana.

What are Chakras and Kundalini?

Like the same electricity runs various appliances, a common form of energy makes our body systems function. However, the energy used for these functions is a fraction of our inner energy that is dormant. Most of us are not aware of it. This energy lay in the form of a coiled snake at the base of the spine in the Mooladhar Chakra. This is called Kundalini Shakti (divine feminine energy). The Kundalini experience is frequently reported as a feeling of electric current running along the spine.

The focus of Chakra Sadhna is to awaken Kundalini through Dhyana, Pranayama, and breathing. Kundalini is an important concept in Shiva Tantra. This energy, when cultivated and awakened through Chakra Sadhna, leads to spiritual liberation.

Normally, a tiny part of this energy flows into other Chakras. Men and women have opposite energies – the positive and negative respectively and the two are complementary. The equal and opposite energies of a man and a woman cause the attraction between them.

The flow of energy is up and down. A small fillip to the wave creates sexual desire and the latent energy manifests in the sexual act. Since Kundalini Shakti is located in the Mooladhar Chakra, it flows downwards. The explosion of energy in this union of two equal and opposite energies leads to procreation.

This energy is the cause behind the Universe. All life forms from humans to plants and animals are engaged in self-preservation. Plants create seeds that will perpetuate the species. A tree is always trying to ensure its seed reaches the soil for germination.

Man is the only species that has learnt to use this energy to attain (sexual) pleasure. All other creatures use this energy only for self-preservation. The man can do this due to his well-developed intellect that other creatures do not have. The use of this energy for sexual pleasure has been the cause of his fall. Man has also manipulated this energy to alleviate himself and for complete transformation.

According to Yoga and Tantra, it is important for the semen to rise to Sahasrara Chakra, thought that science rates as impossible since there is no channel available for the semen to rise up. According to human physiology, semen can fall and not rise. So if one goes by modern science believing this idea may be difficult. However, science has not explored all frontiers; there are many fields that are beyond the logic of science.

As science does not recognise the existence of the soul in humans, it also rejects the concept of semen having a soul or the life energy. Semen has a two-hour life span and if it reaches the ova inside the womb of a woman's body in this time period, life is conceived.

Thus, behind each life conceived is the struggle of lakhs of sperms to reach the ova. This explains why sperms move very fast. There is only one winner in the end and the rest perish. At times, even a single sperm may not reach the ova in time, conception happens rarely.

There has to be a difference between the winner and the rest.

Till it is alive, a sperm has a body and a soul. In two hours, the energy vanishes turning it into a dead material. So, its body is like a vehicle that moves to carry the soul in the form of energy. From the perspective of spirituality, it is the energy that makes the sperm alive.

Since one part of semen is the energy it can rise. Also, energy does not need any channel to rise. If it was only a body, it would always fall. When this energy meets the ova it leads to the creation of a new life. Therefore, the same energy can rises to Sahasrara Chakra without any physical channcl.

The main purpose of Chakra Sadhna is not to let the energy flow downwards and instead divert it upwards. It is a revolutionary process. Sexual pleasure is a glimpse of the bliss that can happen inside us on the union of the male and female energies.

Both the man and a woman have a male and a female form inside them. We can reach the state of ecstasy with the union of the inner male and female forms. This process does not need a sexual union. Even a celibate, following Brahmacharya, can experience it. In this process, the consciousness merges with cosmic consciousness.

Our brain contains a ductless gland called the Pineal gland. When the flow of energy move up towards Crown Chakra, the Pineal gland releases a secretion called Amrit (elixir of life). It falls from the skull into the Yogi's throat. After he tastes it, he can bring about desired changes in his body. The process is called Kayakalp. He can slow down body ageing. Devraha Baba had reached this stage of his spiritual journey and no wonder he lived for 250 years. The elixir makes a person fully awake and conscious entity; he gets the knowledge of the ultimate truth beyond which there is nothing. Many ancients text of Hindus term this ultimate truth as Satyam-Shivam-Sundaram. It means this truth is Shiva and Shiva is the ultimate beauty.

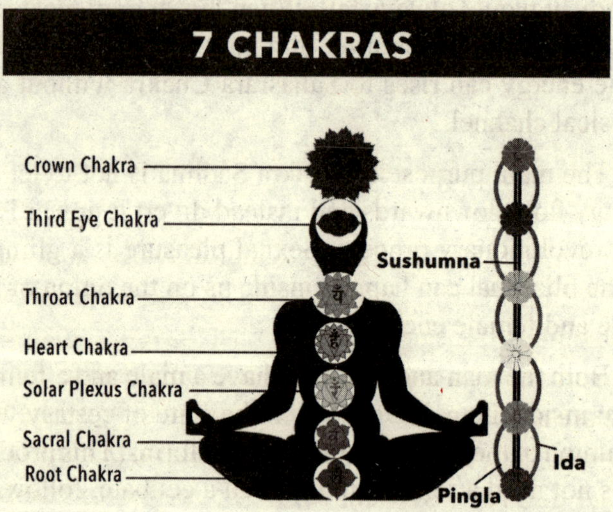

Chakra Sadhna begins with Mooladhar Chakra (Root Chakra) located between testicles and rectum. As it is clear by the name of this Chakra, this is the foundation of our all structures of different dimensions. This Chakra is linked to the Prithvi Tatva in our breath. Prithvi Tatva plays a key role in our physical development. Through Sadhna of Root Chakra, one can steer energy upwards. Over this lay Sacral Chakra (Swadhishthan Chakra) that is linked to Jal Tatva. Sadhna of this Chakra is crucial for moving further in one's Chakra Sadhna.

To activate divine energy (Kundalini Shakti) one must focus on the Sadhna of Root Chakra and Sacral Chakra. Sadhna on these Chakras is relatively easy. The real challenge happens at Solar Plexus Chakra (Manipoorak Chakra) at the navel. Since all 24 Nadis originate from here, a cluster of Nadis at this spot obstructs the flow of energy. The cluster acts like a valve that prevents the upward flow and pushes it down. It is for this joint that usually the energy flows down in our body.

Solar Plexus Chakra is linked to Agni Tatva. Symbolically, the Lanka King Ravana was killed by Rama's arrow that hit him at the navel. Ravana personifies the ego that comes between a human being and his reach to the Divine. We will only realise this after we are able to steer the flow of energy beyond the Solar Plexus Chakra. This step makes us realise that the Divine is no different from our soul. The feeling of one being different from the Divine is the source of our ego.

A Yogi has to work the hardest at the Solar Plexus Chakra. If he manages to move even a tiny part of his energy up to Heart Chakra (Anahata Chakra) he would get a faint glimpse of the Divine and all his doubts will go away. He would begin to understand that Atma, the soul, is not a being; it is a part of the Divine. Musical notes of the divine reverberate inside him as he rises to a state of blissfulness.

Anahata is made of 'Ana' meaning without and 'Aahata' means the sound of the collision. Sound is always created when two objects strike. In this case, the sound is generated without the two objects colliding. Anahata is the only sound that's generated without a collision. It is also called Omkar or Anahata Nad and this phenomenon takes place at Anahat Chakra. It is called Shashwat Vani meaning the eternal sound.

Guru Nanak Dev has spoken about this so simply: "Ek Nam Satnam...Omkar..." there is only one name, pure name and that's the sound of Om. Whosoever can utter it is blessed.

Om is the common link of all major religions. It is not a word but a sound that was reverberating in the universe even before the creation happened. The sound precedes religions.

Om is used differently used by people across the world in their respective linguistic contexts. In the English language, words like Omnipotent and Omniscient are linked to Om. Who can be more powerful or knowledgeable than God? In Semitic religions every prayer said is closed by the recitation of "amen'. The Sikhs say 'Omkar'; Jains, Hindus and Buddhists say 'Om'. The original sound of the Universe has thus been adopted by different religions and languages in their own way.

When the energy reaches Heart Chakra (Anahata Chakra) and activates it, Omkar Nad (sound of omkar) is released. Just think of it; a sound that you are not familiar with is generated inside you! Would you find any object in the world more incredible than it? After this experience, it is natural for you to realise the worthlessness of all material objects. Once a Yogi is able to trigger his Heart Chakra, his only aim is to move ahead in his inner journey towards godliness.

The energy reaches the Heart Chakra after negotiating through obstruction around Solar Plexus Chakra. Like the opening of a clogged drain, this removes memories of our past births and refines our mind. When the energy reaches thc Throat Chakra (Vishudha Chakra) the person acquires the extraordinary qualities of a writer, poet and orator. The unschooled saints wrote the classic after attaining this stage in Chakra Sadhna. They became fine orators like Sant Kabir and Rahim; their spoken word is now rated as classic and taught in schools and universities.

When the energy reaches Throat Chakra and activates it, the practitioner's pure consciousness clears up and he is on the way to attain higher knowledge. Thereafter his oratory is not subservient to the known connotations of words and languages. His words have a unique meaning.

Now onwards, the journey is about steering the flow of energy to the Third Eye Chakra (Agya Chakra) located right in the middle of the brows. One who is able to reach it becomes a Yogi.

The Third Eye Chakra is the meeting point of Ida, Pingla and Sushumna. The Nadis are tied in a knot here.

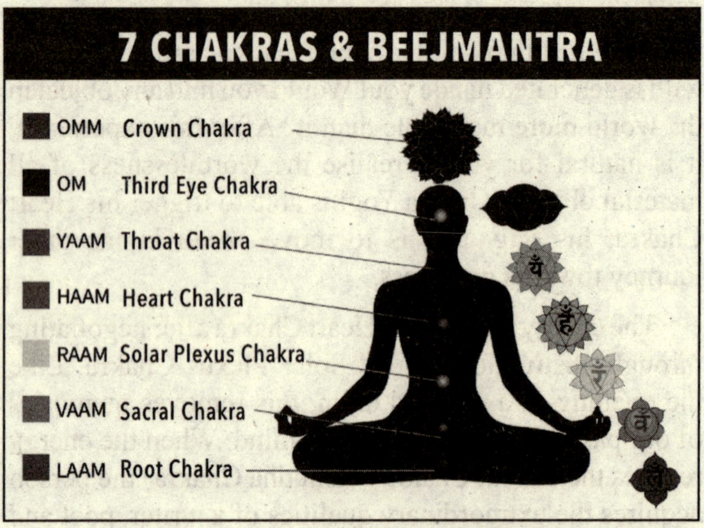

When the Yogi is able to untie the knot at a speed, his Third Eye opens and he acquires celestial powers. He can see the past and the future clearly. The Third Eye is also called the sixth sense. With the help of the Third Eye, a Yogi will be able to open the tenth gate of the body – Brahmarandra.

Here is a simple method to practice Chakra Sadhna and it must be done only after learning Pranayama from a Yoga teacher.

Sit in Vajrasan or Siddhasan – spine upright and neck slightly bent. Check your Nadi even though the Sadhna can be done in any Nadi's phase. Inhale deeply and exhale fully for five minutes. Thereafter, keep the focus on Chakras, one by one, starting with Root Chakra and moving to Sacral Chakra, Solar Plexus Chakra, Heart Chakra, Throat Chakra and Third Eye Chakra.

At each Chakra recite mantras at least five times. Inhale to your full capacity. Focus on Root Chakra. Slowly breathe out while reciting the 'Laam mantra' with uttering 'Laa' sound during exhalation and 'M' while inhalation. While reciting 'M' syllabi, shift the focus on Third Eye Chakra. After exhalation, shrink your rectum inside and hold your breath as long as possible. During this, keep the focus on the Third Eye Chakra and recite a mantra five times in five breaths.

After practising this for a few days, you will feel the energy rise from Root Chakra. Reverberations in the spine and spasms in the navel are clues to its activation. Do remember that we do not have to produce any sound but experience the sounds while breathing.

Likewise, one can do Sadhna of all other Chakras with the specific mantra. Sacral Chakra goes with Vaam mantra, Solar Plexus Chakra with Ram, Heart Chakra with Yaam, Throat Chakra with Haam and Third Eye Chakra with Om. Points to be kept in mind:

1. Begin recitation of mantra while exhaling.
2. Keep the focus on the Chakra as you recite the mantra.

3. And while exhaling when it comes to recitation of the last syllabi 'M' keep the focus on the Third Eye Chakra.
4. Shrink your rectum in and hold your breath as long as possible.
5. Thereafter, inhale fully and begin the second round of recitation.

After some practice, you will be able to feel the flow of energy and make out the Chakra on which your energy is residing. This will enable you to move ahead in Chakra Sadhna.

How does this work? When we exhale fully, a vacuum is created within our body. So, when we inhale, the air hits hard through Nadi on the particular Chakra. On repetition of this process, the locked-up secretions in the Chakra start oozing leading to activation of Sushumna Nadi and flow of energy. To reverse the normal downward flow of energy the rectum is tightly shrunk to lock the opening and helps in the upward movement of energy.

After the Sadhna, one should keep eyes closed and mind focused on breathing. Basically, you should inspect your breathing to find out the point where incoming breath changes into an outgoing one. You would be able to locate the exact point. Meanwhile, you should continue deep breathing. If you do it successfully, you will surely have a beautiful experience. You will not be able to describe it.

In the end, I request you to first unlearn all you know about Dhyana and Sadhna before embarking on the inner journey.

RECAP

- Our body is like a big city with ten doors. In the Indian tradition of spirituality, these doors are ten openings.
- These doors are the mouth, a set of two each eye, ears and nostrils, reproductive tract opening and the rectum. The tenth gate is located at the top of the skull and is called Brahmarandra. This is the topmost Chakra also called Sahasrara Chakra.
- The discovery of this door is the goal of a yogi. Only on the opening of this door, one can see the Divinity.
- Like the common electric power running all the appliances, our energy runs all functions of our body. However, this energy is not even a fraction of our real energy.
- Our real energy has tremendous power. It lay inert in the area of the navel, Swadhishthan Chakra or between rectum and sperm sac, Mooladhar Chakra. This latent energy is called Kundalini Shakti.
- The purpose of Chakra Sadhna is to stop the downward flow of this energy and push it upwards. The downward flow makes us get sexual pleasure

and this is just a glimpse of the real pleasure we get from the union of man and woman residing inside us.

- Ida is the woman and Pingla the manly manifestation inside us.
- When Sushumna Nadi flows upwards and Ida and Pingla meet at Aagya Chakra, it gives us pleasure that cannot be described in words. This process is also called the opening of the Third Eye or activation of the sixth sense.
- A Yogi thus steers the energy to Sahasrara Chakra and is able to open the tenth gate. At this, his consciousness reaches the celestial level.
- When the energy flows up towards Brahmarandra, the pineal gland in our brain gets activated and releases a secretion called Amrit (elixir) in spiritual science.

❑❑❑

15

CHAPTER

Why The Delay?

By now, you have become familiar with the secrets of breathing and also know that you can achieve all that you always wanted.

The possibilities of achieving happiness, love, peace, spiritual vision are for us to grab in this lifetime. We just have to follow a method.

Impediments often mar our ambitions. Since you know that which Nadi will enable you to achieve your goals in a particular situation, you can practice the do-it-yourself techniques to set things right.

All you need to do is to keep your eye on the Nadi and the Tatva and remember the suitable combinations of Nadi and Tatva for a particular task. It just requires practice and there is no need to memorize anything.

Many of us believe we are a body. However, in reality, we are energy. Scientists also say the universe is made of energy and we being a small part of this universe cannot be different. As per the science of spiritualism, we are energy.

Our breath acts as a regulator of our energy. Since we know the secrets of breathing, we can control our actions as per our needs and desires.

This book has also made you realise about your mind, its strengths and weaknesses; how it is built and rules over us all our life.

You must explore the unlimited power of your mind.

The result will surprise you. You just need to start practising.

Always remember your breath is the most valuable asset with you. After knowing the secrets of breathing there is nothing impossible for you.

Good luck to you.

Request:

As an author, I would really appreciate if you could leave behind a review if you like the book. It will be really helpful.